GW01217751

Who is it ?

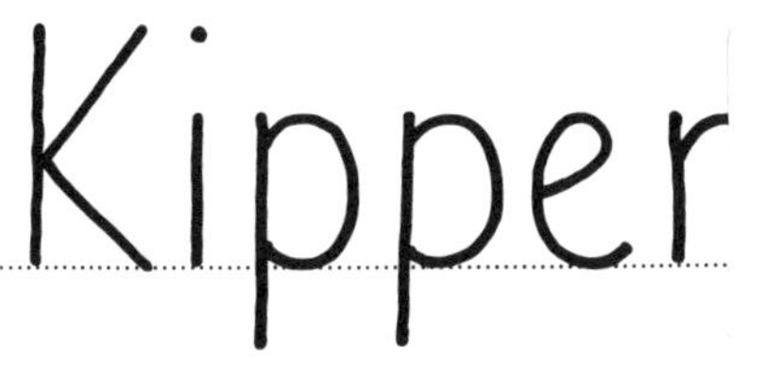
Kipper

RING BOOKS

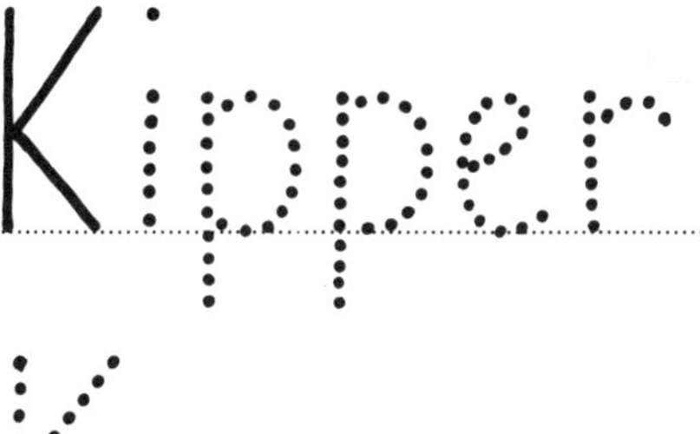
Kipper
K

Biff

Biff

B

Chip

Chip

C

Who is it ?

Floppy the dog

Floppy the dog

F

Mum

Mum

M

Dad

Dad

D

Join up the same **first** letters.

p
t
p
t

Join up the same **first** letters.

l
n
Santa Claus
The North Pole
The World.
l
n

First letters

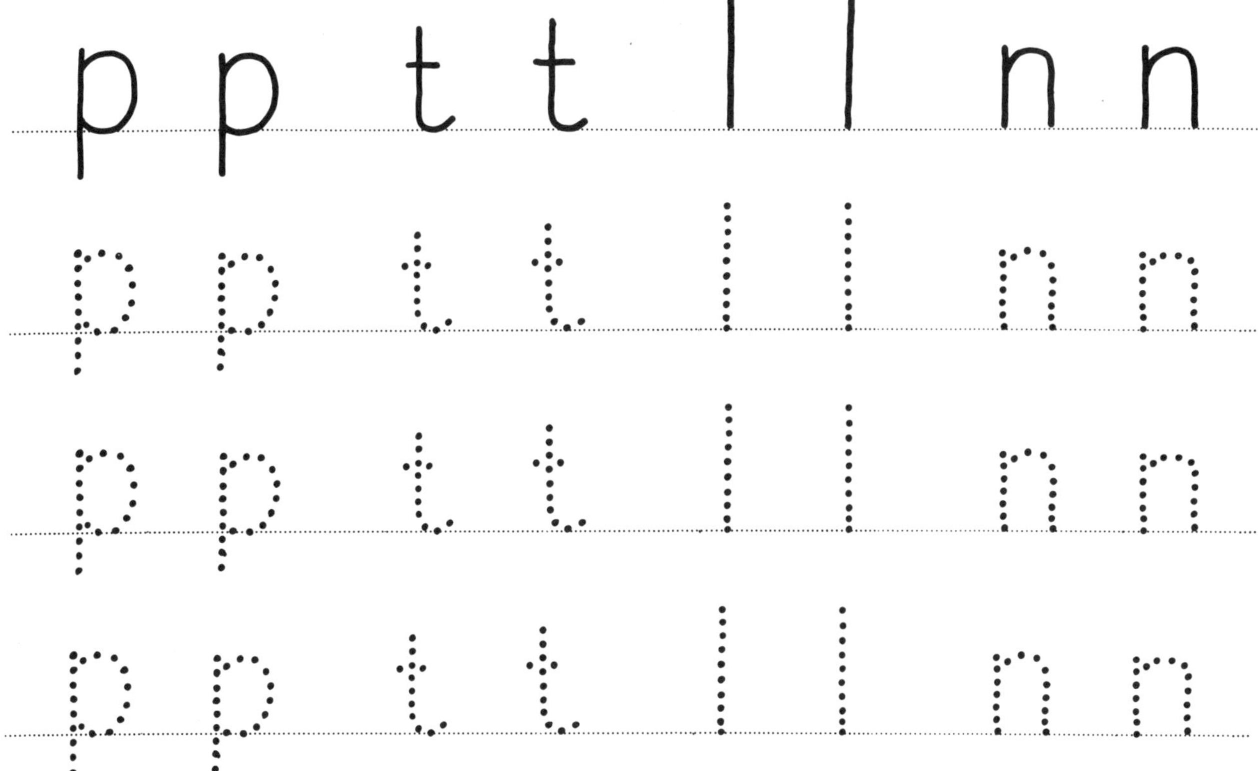
p p t t l l n n

Join up the same **first** letters.

p t l n

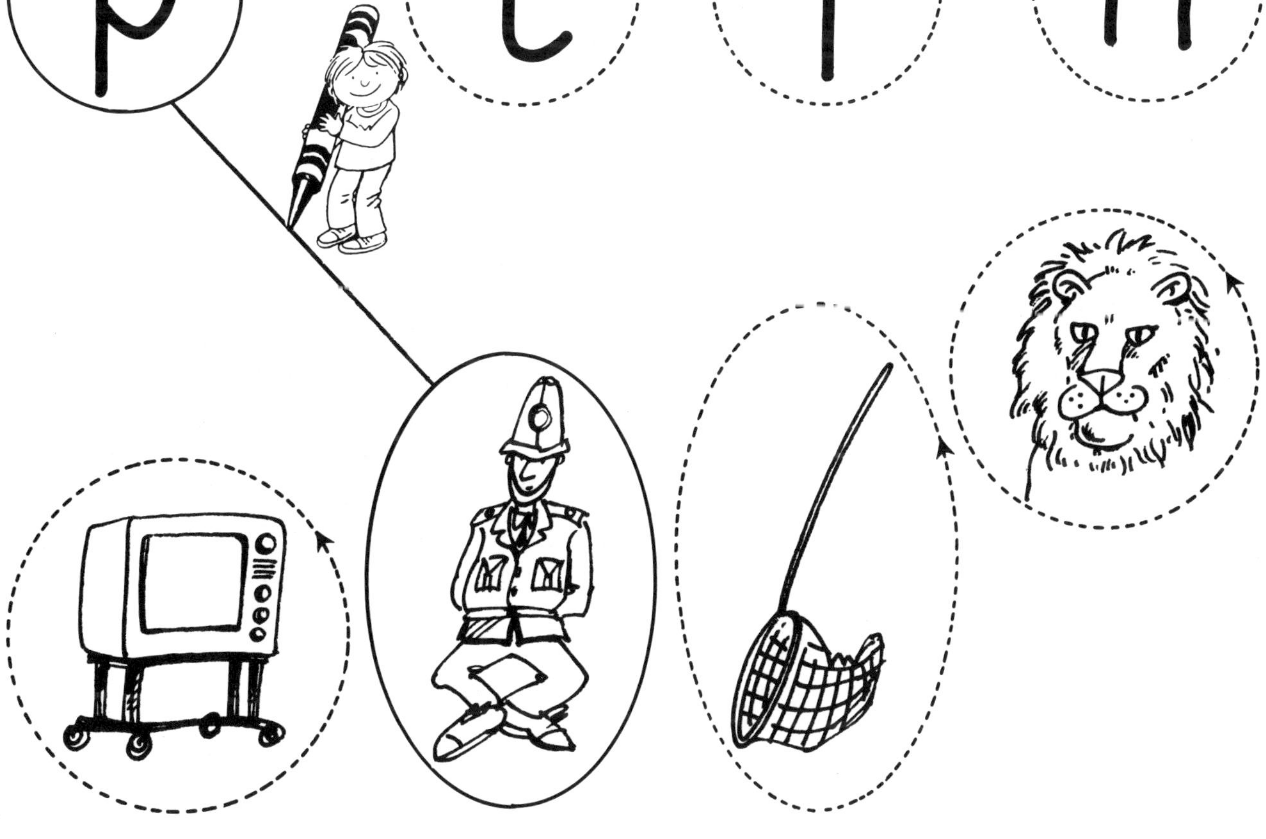

Copy the words.

They wanted a dog.

They wanted a dog.

T w a d .

Everyone got Floppy.

Everyone got Floppy.

E g F .

Copy the words.

Chip pushed.

Chip pushed.

Chip .

Biff pulled.

Biff pulled.

Biff .

They put in Floppy.

They put in Floppy.

They Floppy.

A.8

Join up the same **first** letters.

b

m

b

m

Join up the same **first** letters.

g

c

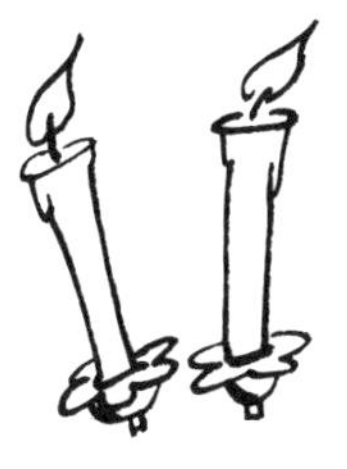

g

c

First letters

b b m m c c g g

b b m m c c g g

b b m m c c g g

b b m m c c g g

Join up the same **first** letters.

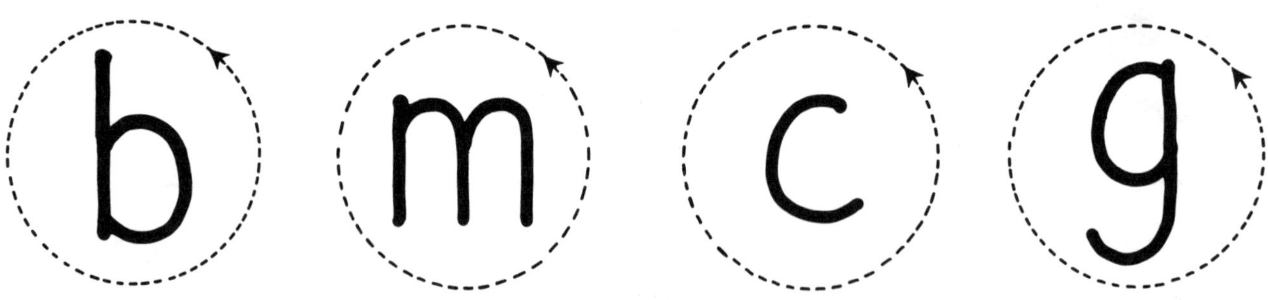

b
m
c
g

✓ X

'Everyone stop it!' said Mum. ☐

Dad went to stop it. ☐

'He got cross,' said Biff. ☐

'I made Mum cross,' said Dad. ☐

Dad had got cross. ☐

'It was the dog,' they said. ☐

Join up the same **first** letters.

d
k
d
k

Join up the same **first** letters.

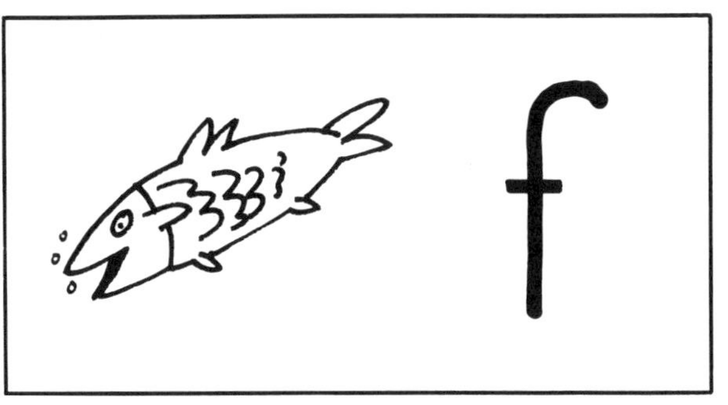

f

s

f

HERE
THERE

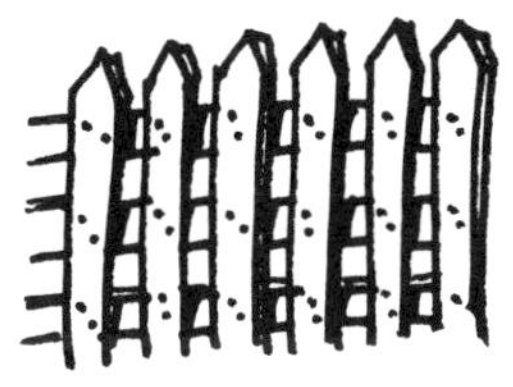

s

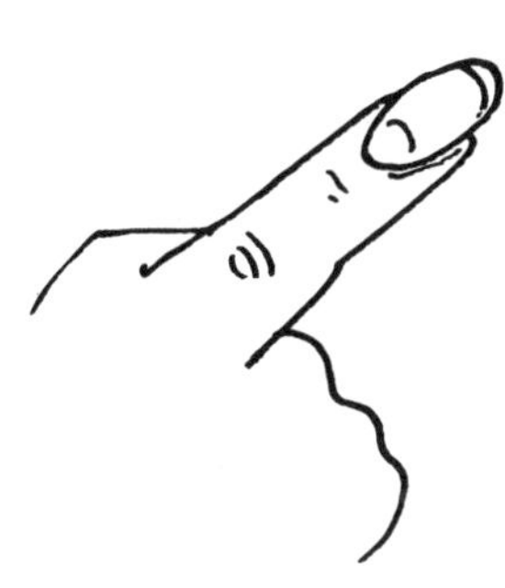

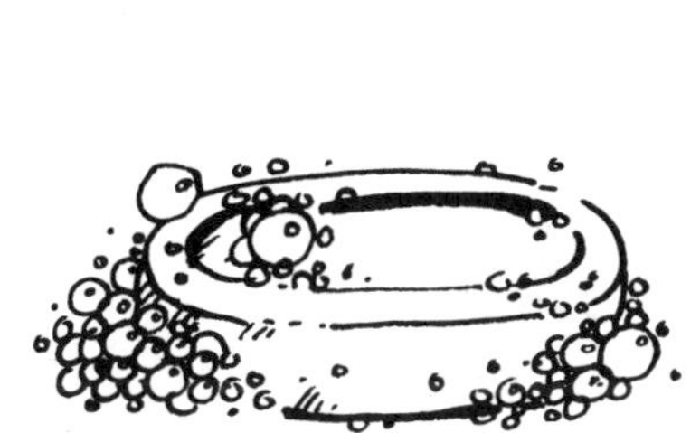

First letters

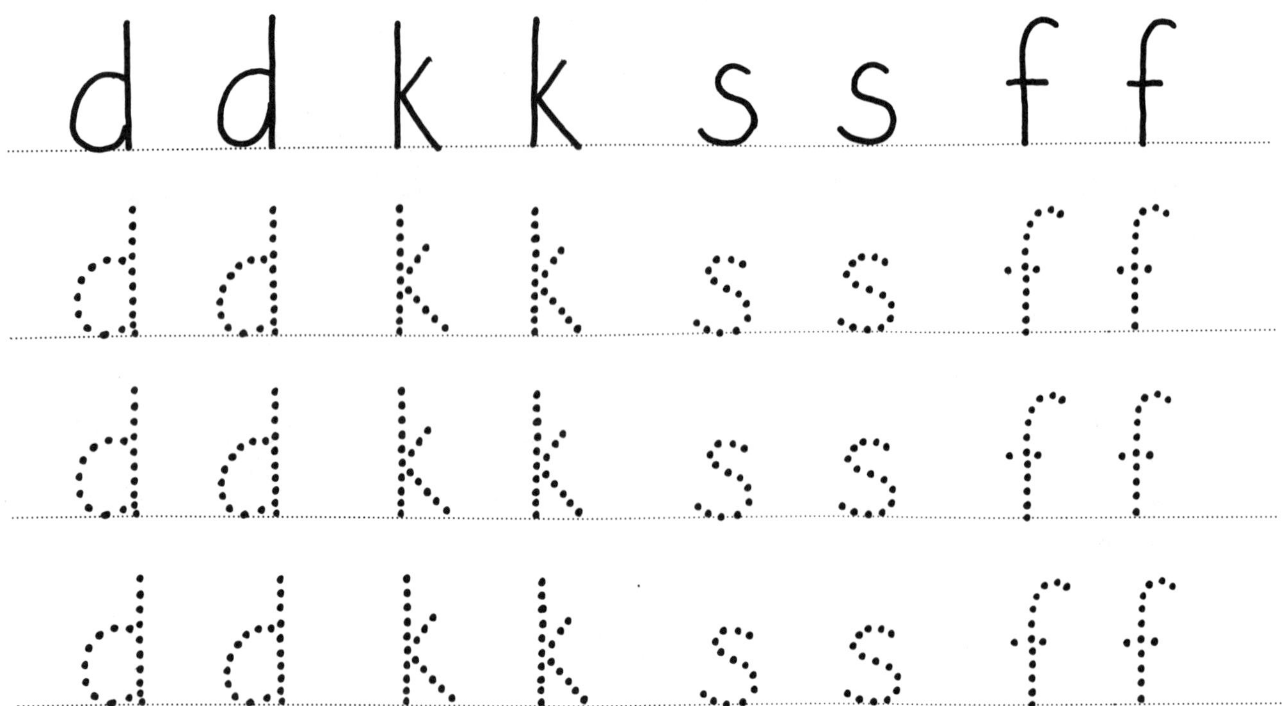
d d k k s s f f

Join up the same **first** letters

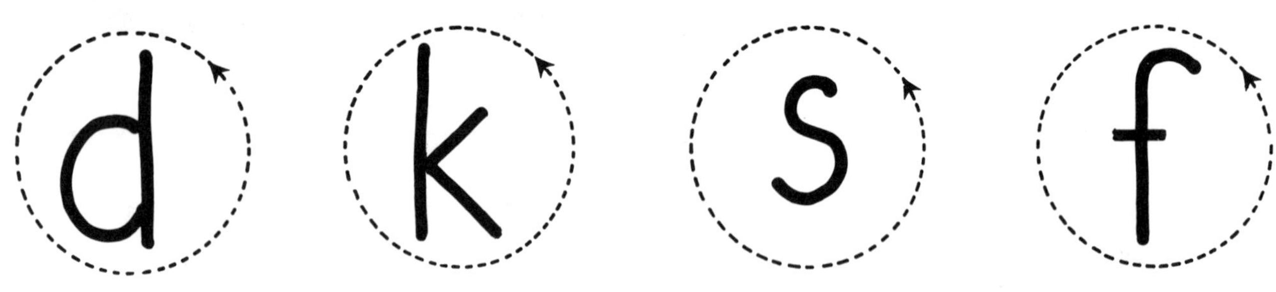
d
k
s
f

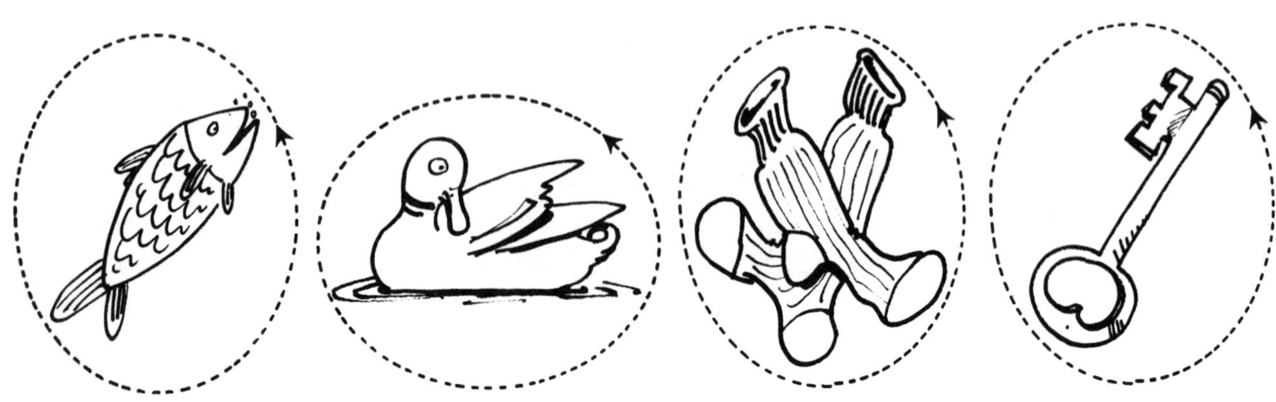

Who was it?

Join up.

Who said stop?

Who got cross?

Who pushed?

Who pulled?

Who had to stop?

Who was it?

Chip, Biff, Dad, everyone, Kipper, Mum.

Who was cross?

It was ....

Who made Kipper a  ?

It was ....

Who put Floppy in the  ?

It was ....

Who went in the  ?

I w ....

✓ X

I am Wilma.
He is Wilf.
Floppy barked.
Biff jumped down.
Wilma couldn't get on.
I climbed up the tree.

✓ X

Get down, Floppy!

☐

Everyone looked at Dad.

☐

It is what I wanted.

☐

The children played.

☐

I couldn't get it.

☐

Chip had made a rug. He gave it to Mum.

☐

Join up the same **first** letters.

r

j

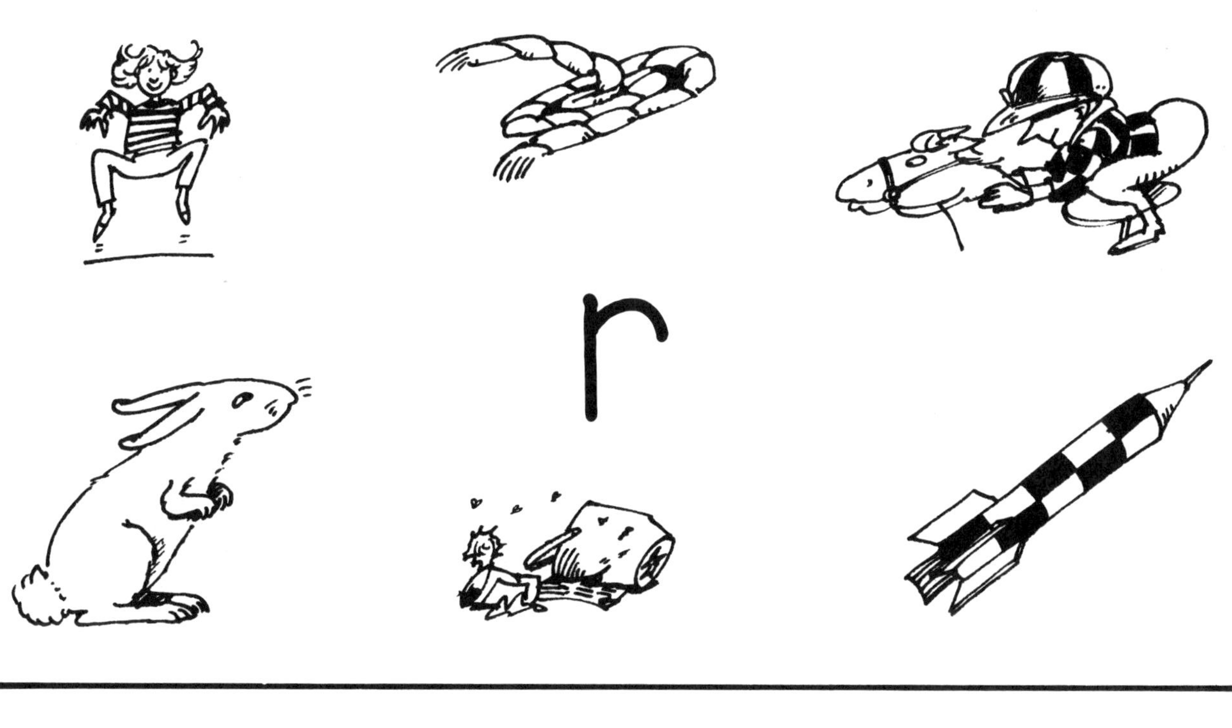
r

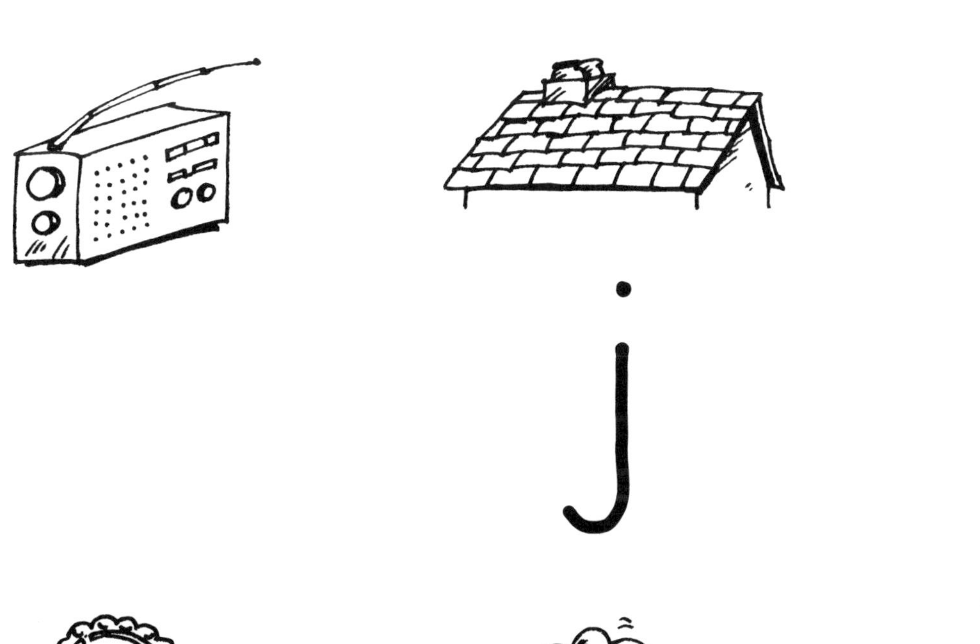
j

B.4

Join up the same **first** letters.

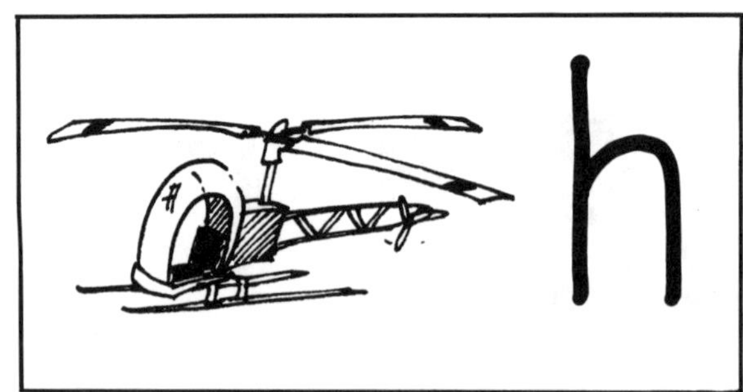

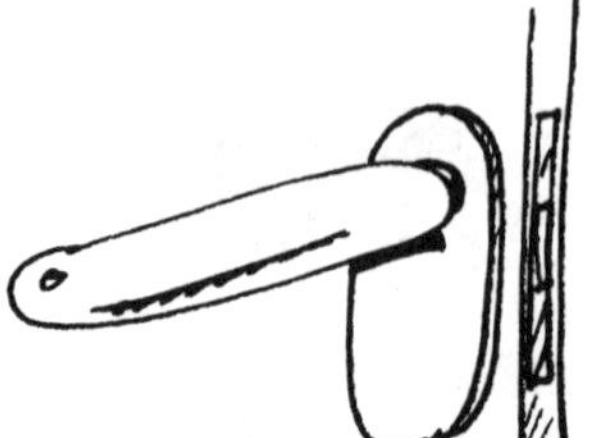

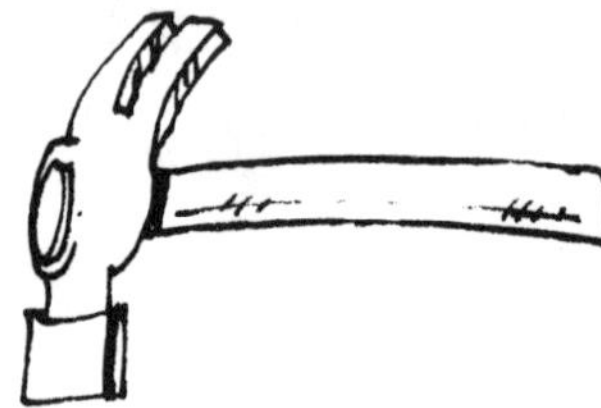

h

First letters

r r w w h h j j

Join up the same **first** letters.

r w h j

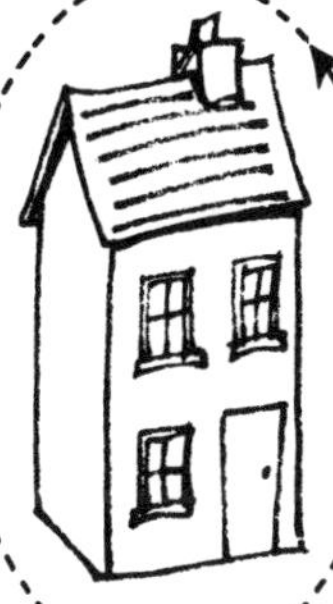

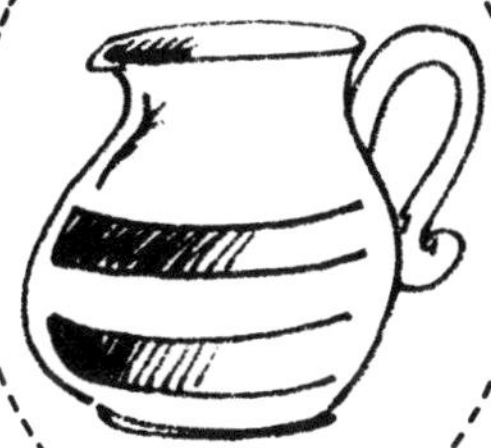

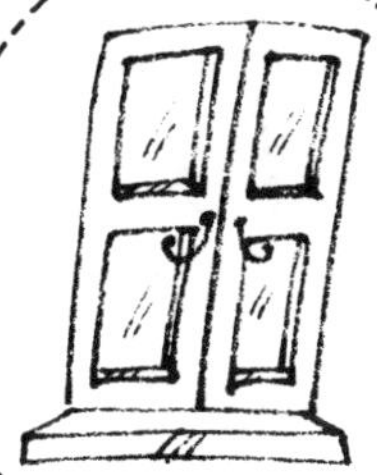

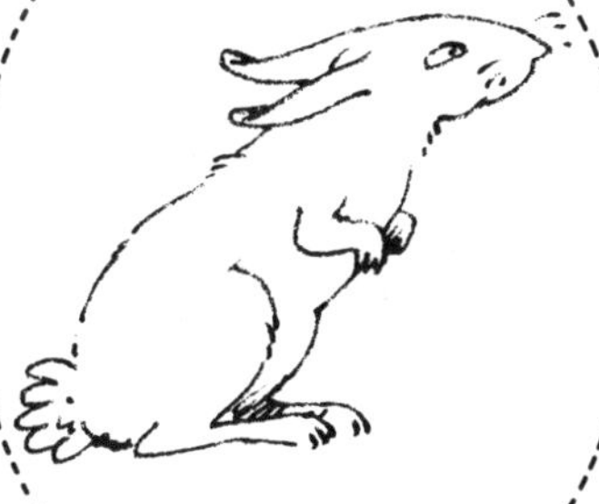

Capital letters

c C c C c C c C

c C c C

o O o O

p P p P

s S s S

u U u U

v V v V

w W w W

x X x X

Join up the same **first** letters.

qu

v

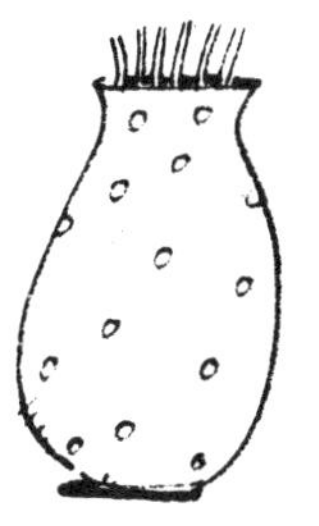

qu

v

B.8

Join up the same **first** letters.

z

y

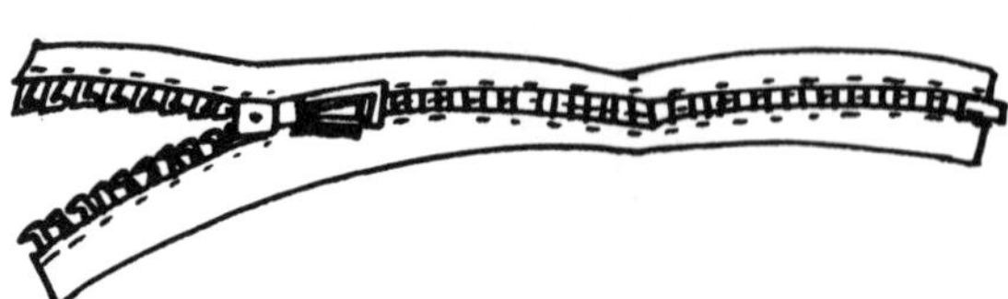

z

y

First letters

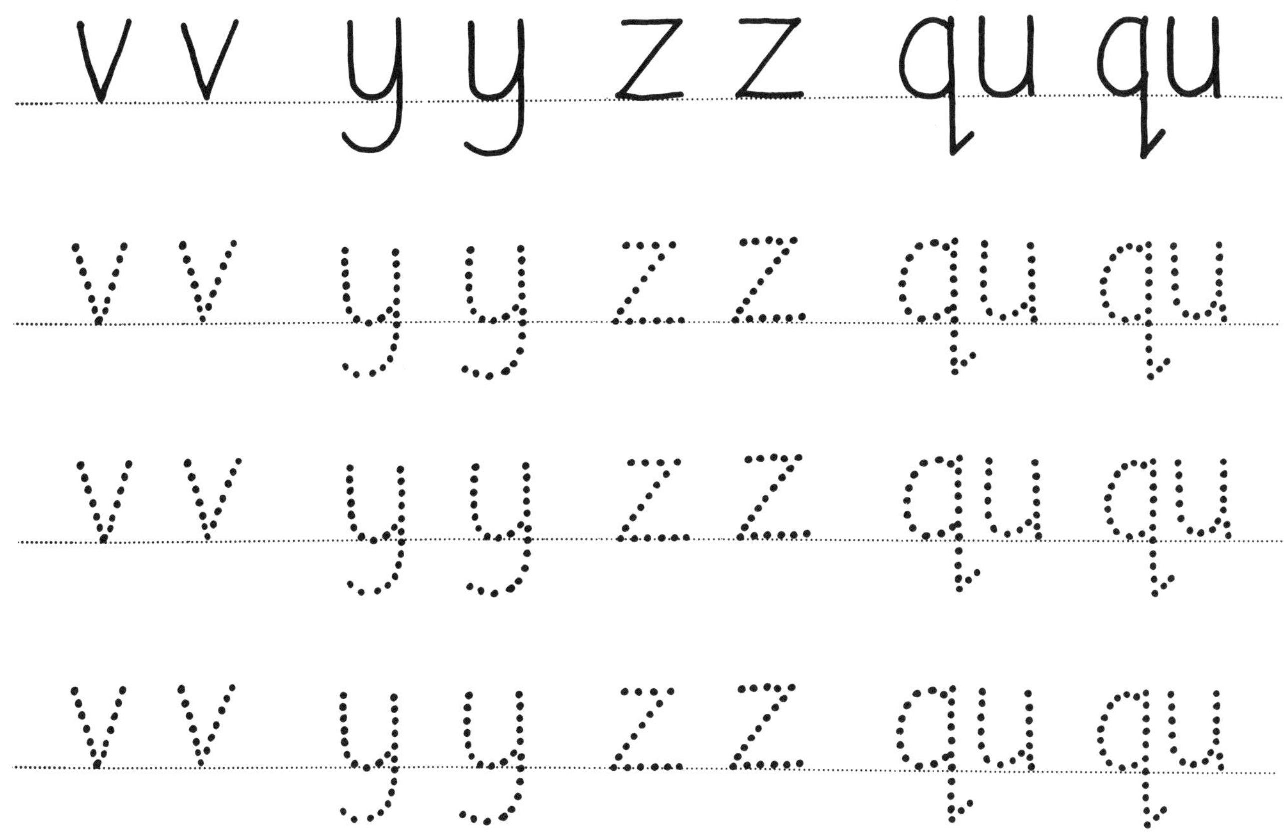
v v y y z z qu qu
v v y y z z qu qu
v v y y z z qu qu
v v y y z z qu qu

Join up the same **first** letters.

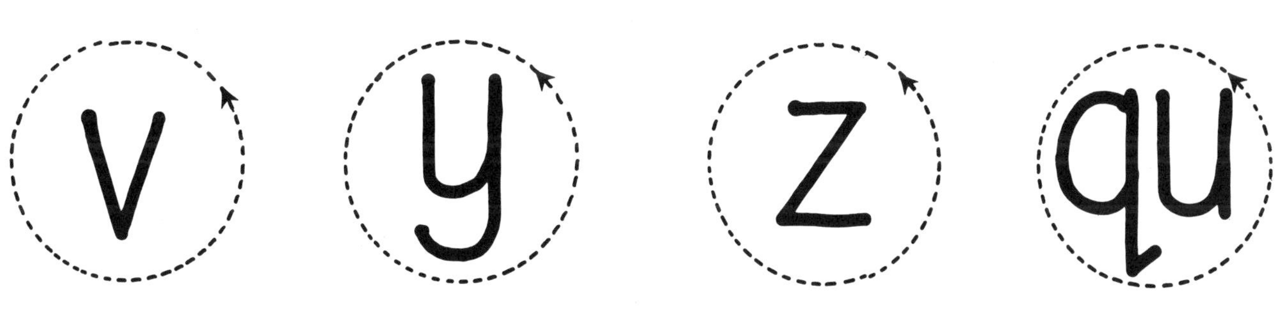
v
y
z
qu

Capital letters

z Z z Z

i I i I

k K k K

m M m M

f F f F

l L l L

j J j J

y Y y Y

n N n N

Join up the same **first** letters.

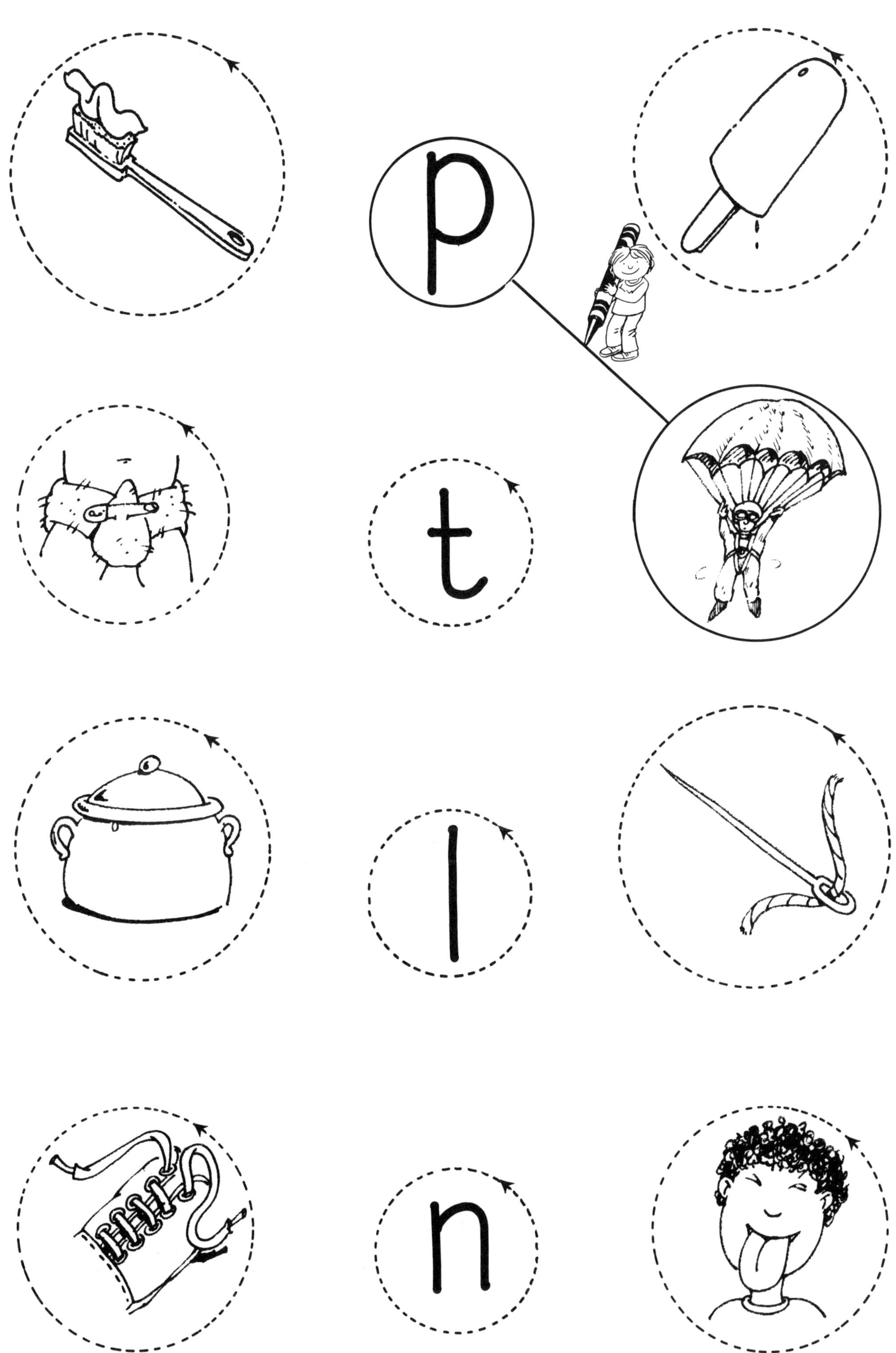
p
t
l
n

Join up the same **first** letters.

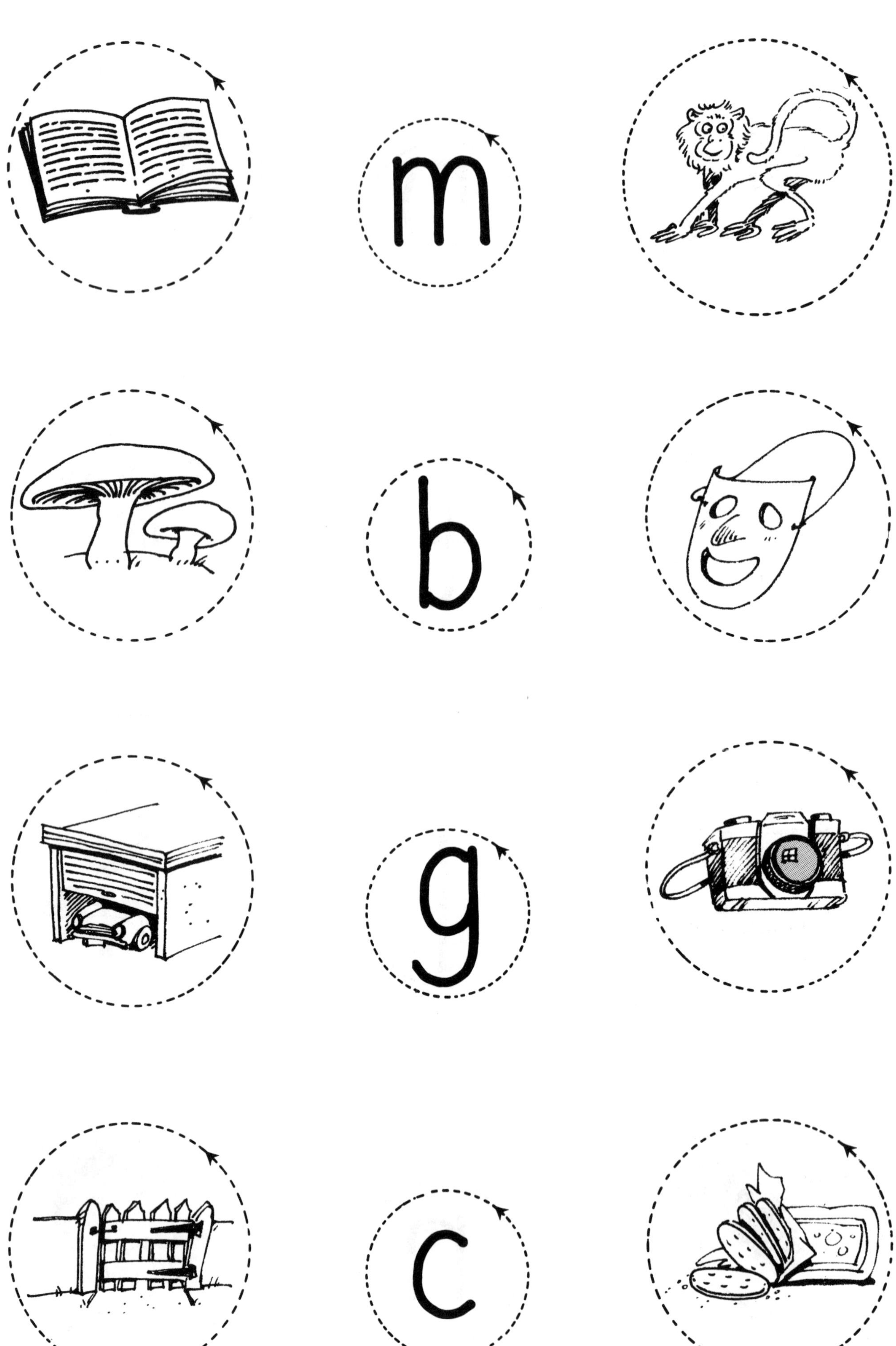
m
b
g
c

B.13

Join up the same **first** letters.

d
k
f
s

Capital letters

h H h H

b B b B

t T t T

d D d D

q Q q Q

r R r R

g G g G

a A a A

e E e E

Join up the same **first** letters.

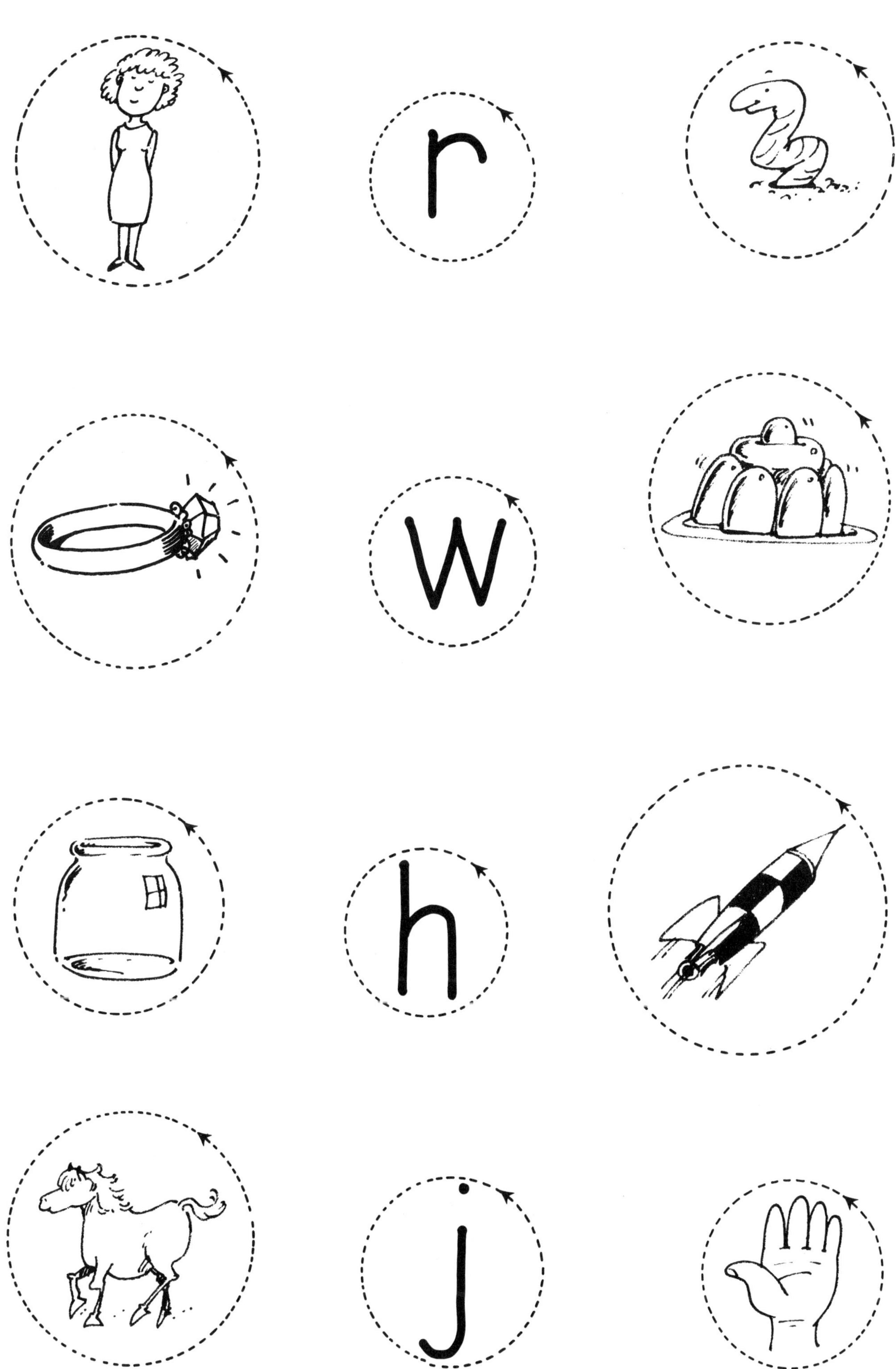
r
w
h
j

Join up the same **first** letters.

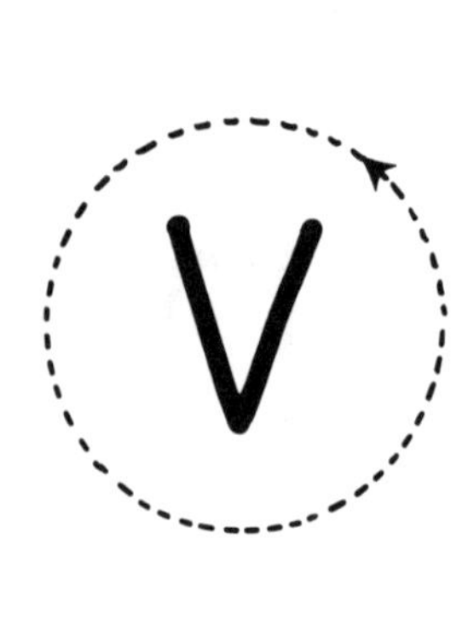
v

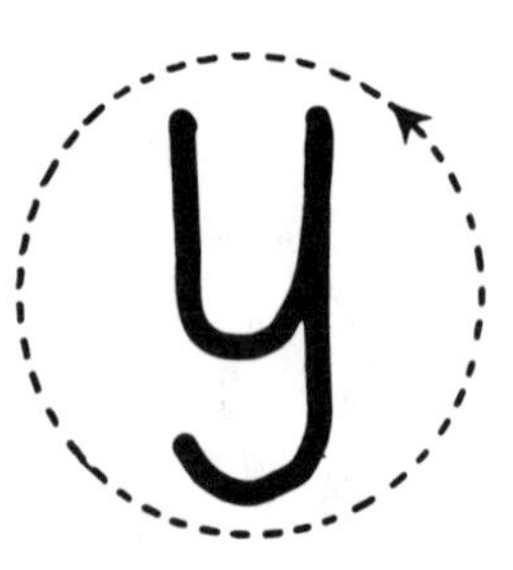
y

z

qu

✓ ×

Dad and Mum wanted
wallpaper for the house. ☑
Mum and Dad were outside. ☑

It was for the outside. ☐
It was for the big room. ☐

They looked at the wallpaper. ☐
They liked this. ☐

Mum liked this wallpaper. ☐
Dad liked this wallpaper. ☐

Ring the **first** letter.

p t l n b m g c

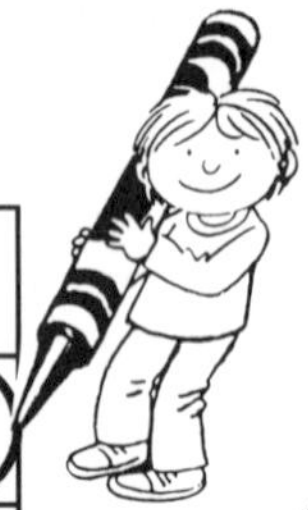

p t l n b m g c

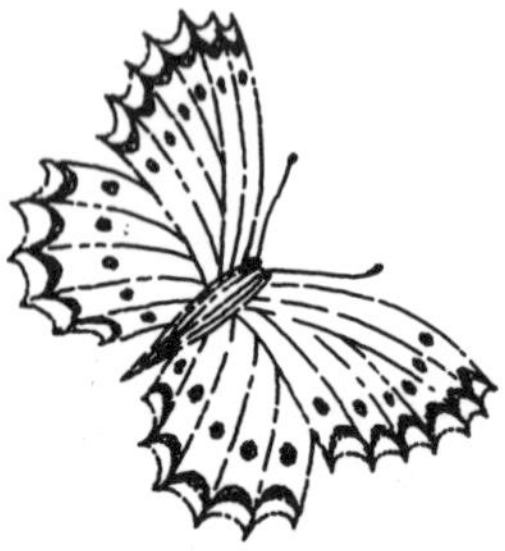

p t l n b m g c

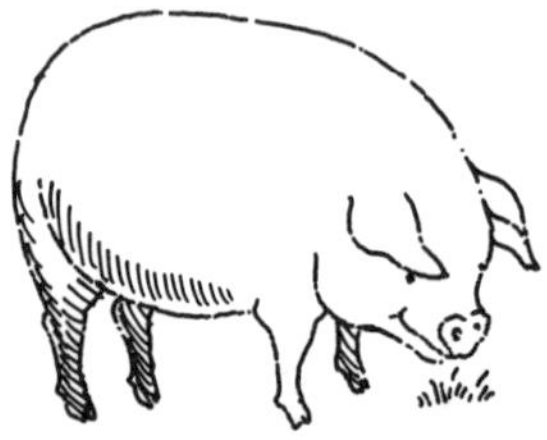

p t l n b m g c

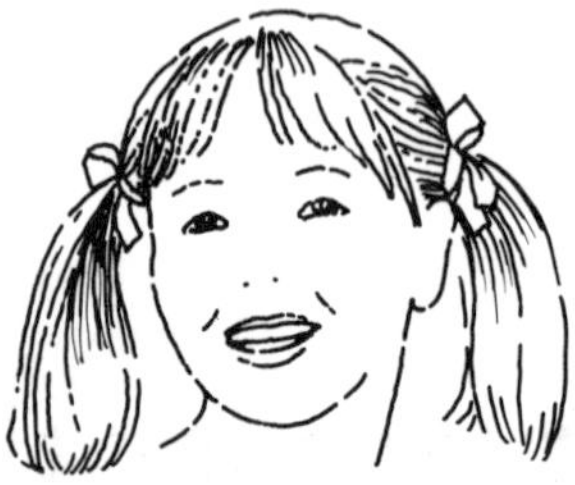

p t l n b m g c

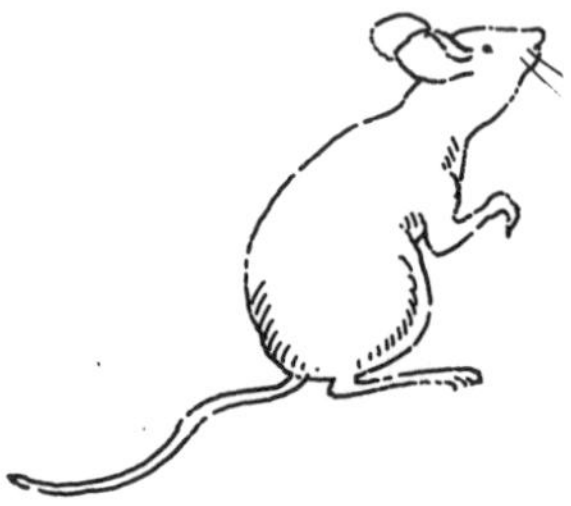

p t l n b m g c

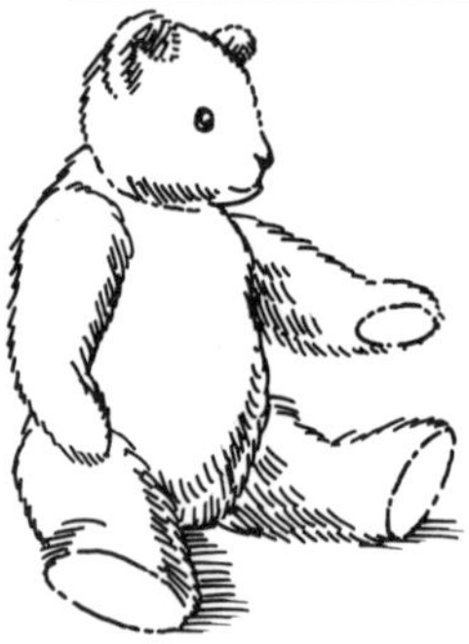

p t l n b m g c

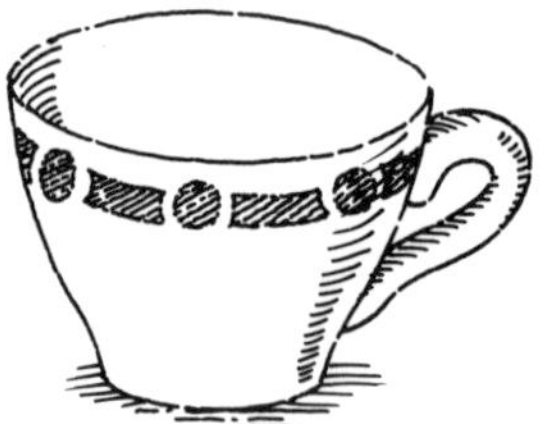

p t l n b m g c

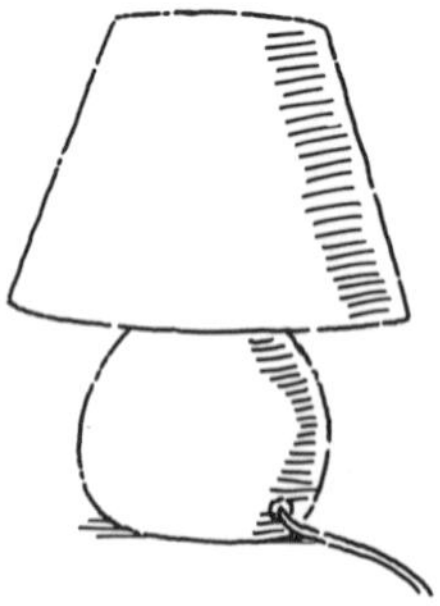

p t l n b m g c

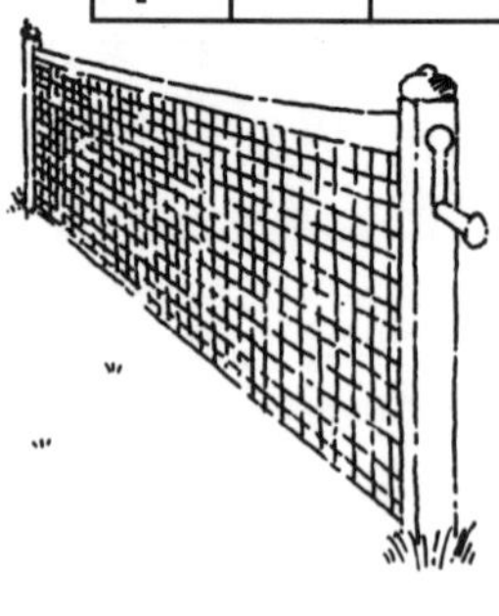

p t l n b m g c

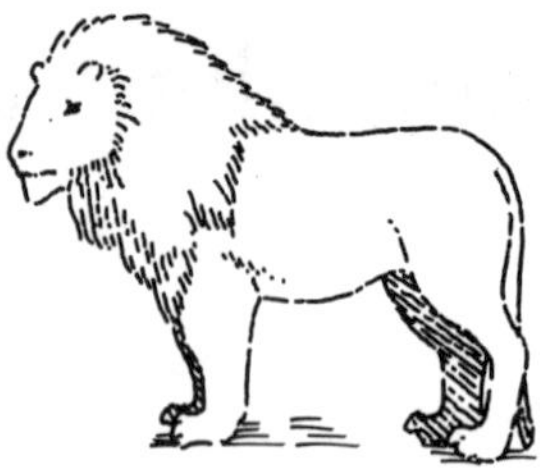

p t l n b m g c

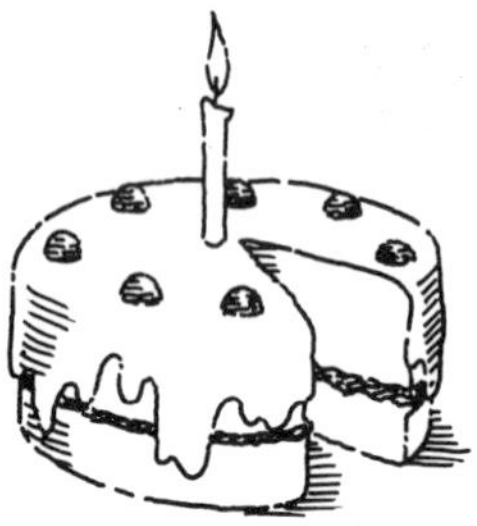

p t l n b m g c

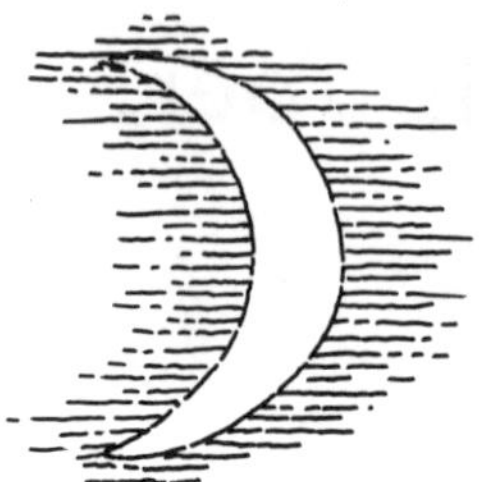

p t l n b m g c

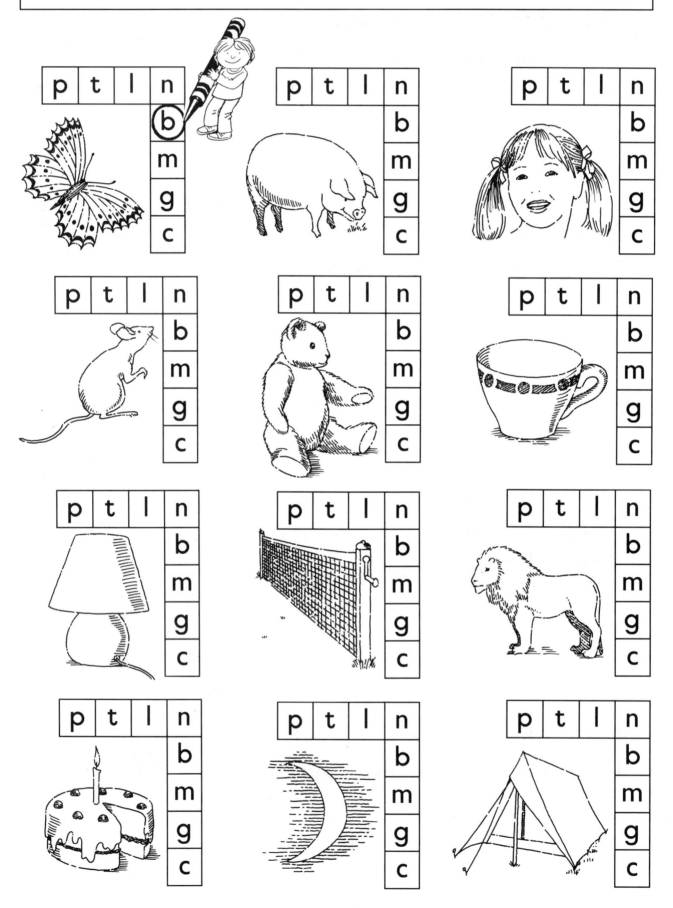

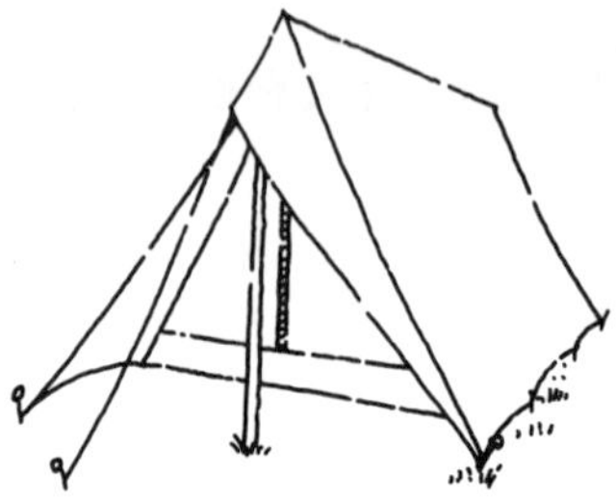

Biff came outside. ☐
A man pulled up outside. ☐

'Come in!' said Biff. ☐
He came with a box. ☐

Biff helped get a box down. ☐
Biff came to play. ☐

Biff helped put things in a box. ☐
The man helped with a box. ☐

The man came outside. ☐
Biff came outside to play. ☐

Ring the **first** letter.

d	k	f	s	r	w	h	j

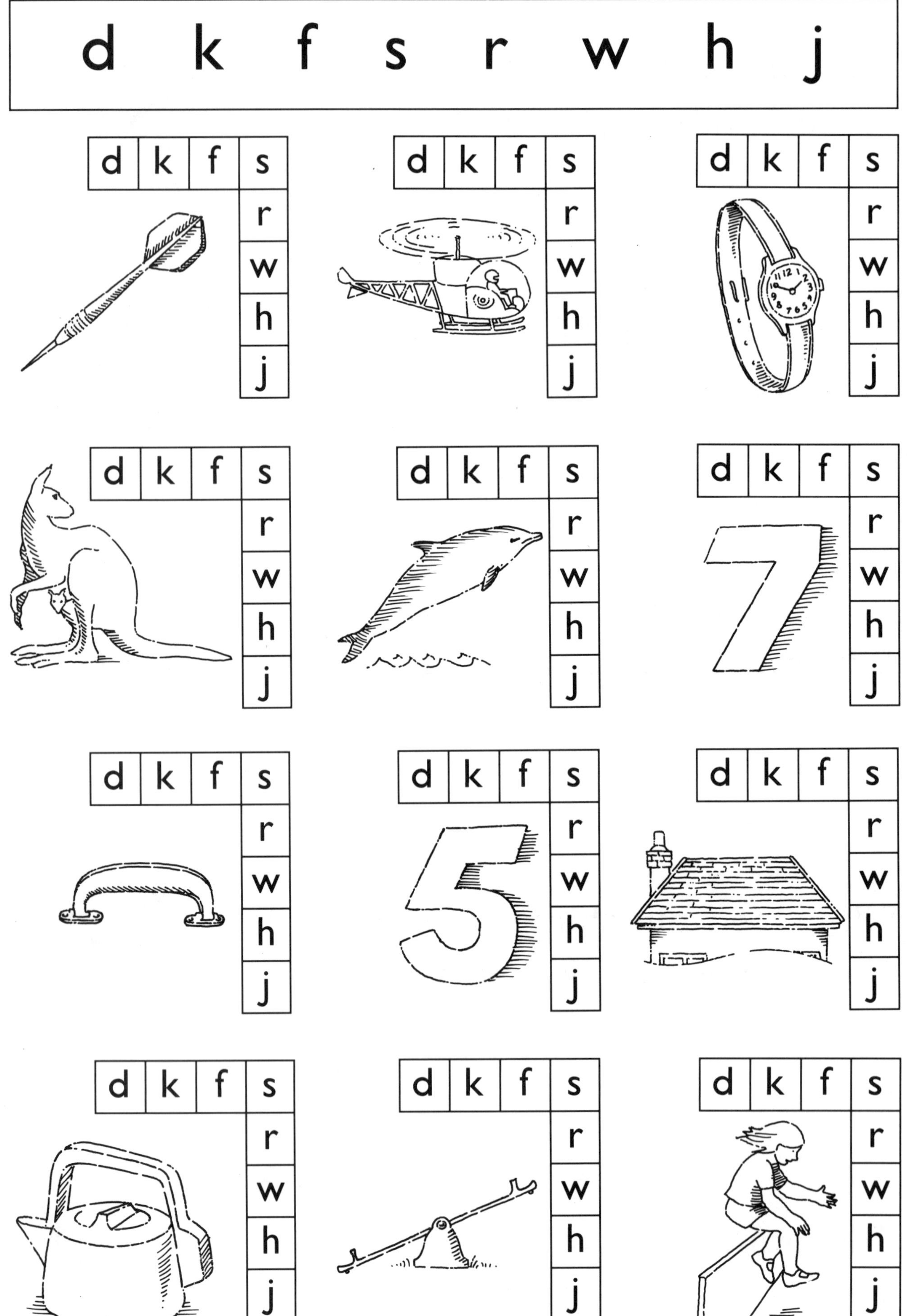
d k f s r w h j
d k f s r w h j
d k f s r w h j
d k f s r w h j
d k f s r w h j
d k f s r w h j
d k f s r w h j
d k f s r w h j
d k f s r w h j
d k f s r w h j
d k f s r w h j
d k f s r w h j

✓ ×

Wilma painted the door. ☐
Wilma opened the door. ☐

Wilma went inside. ☐
Wilf went inside. ☐

Wilma found a little box. ☐
Wilf found a little box. ☐

Wilf played. ☐
Wilma painted. ☐

Wilma painted. ☐
Wilma looked at the time. ☐

Ring the **first** letter.

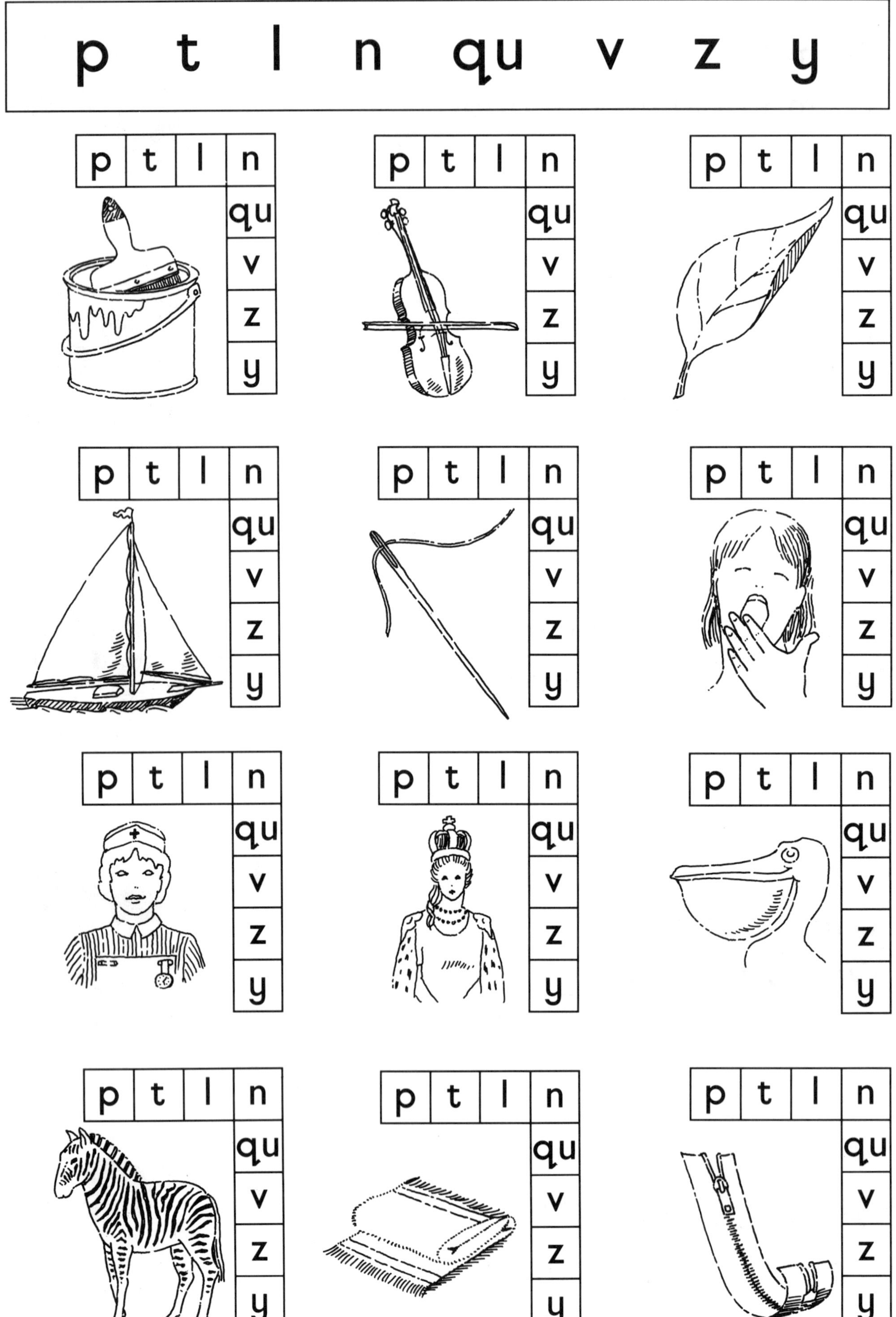
p t l n qu v z y

✓ ×

The storm was inside. ☐
The children looked at the storm. ☐

There is a witch up there. ☐
The witch had come down. ☐

The witch jumped down. ☐
The witch came inside. ☐

They helped with her things. ☐
The children had a key. ☐

The witch mended it. ☐
The children painted it. ☐

C.8

Ring the **first** letter.

b	m	g	c	r	w	h	j

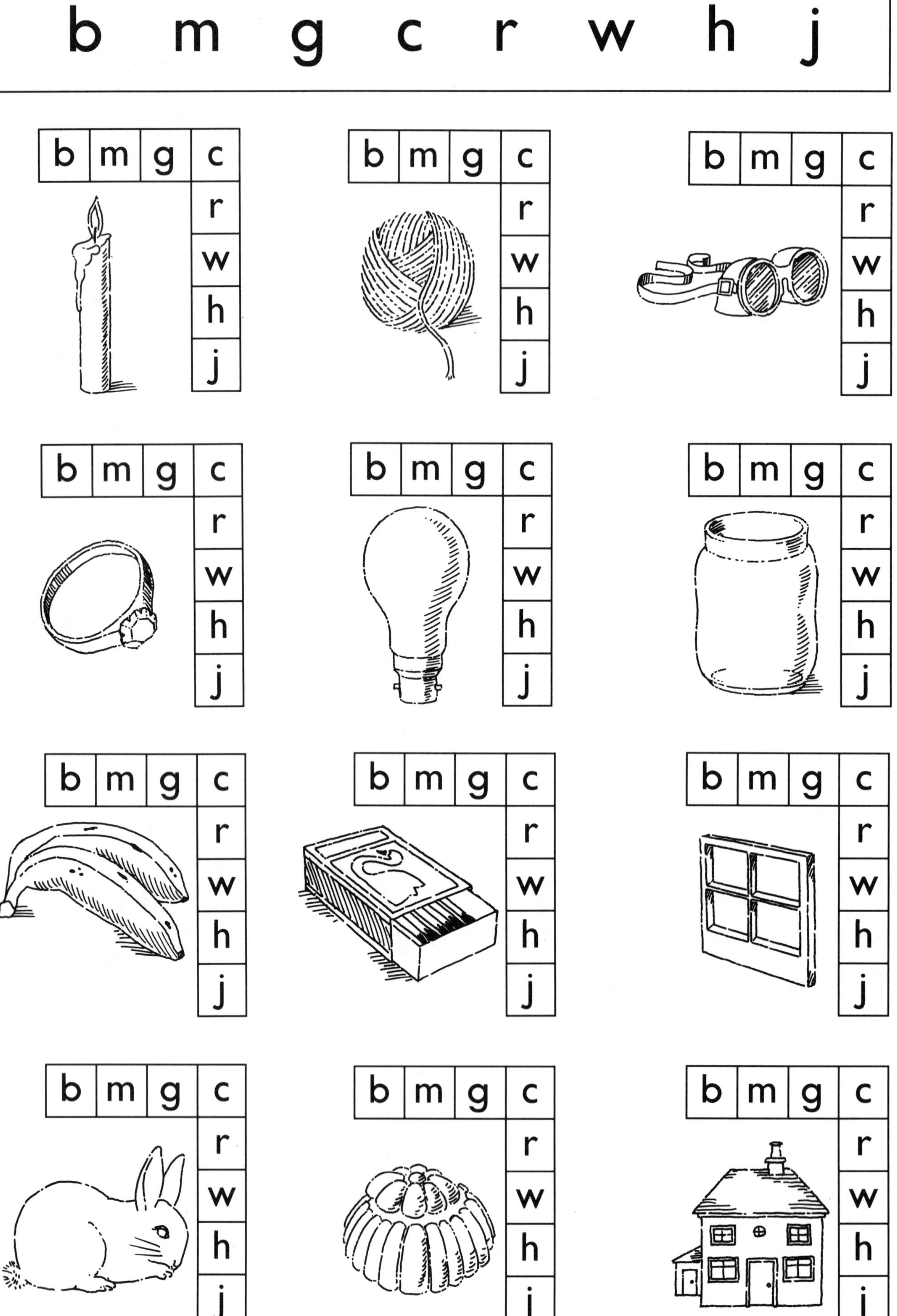
b m g c r w h j
b m g c r w h j
b m g c r w h j
b m g c r w h j
b m g c r w h j
b m g c r w h j
b m g c r w h j
b m g c r w h j
b m g c r w h j
b m g c r w h j
b m g c r w h j
b m g c r w h j

Put in the **first** letter.

m	c	g	d	k	f	s	r	w	h

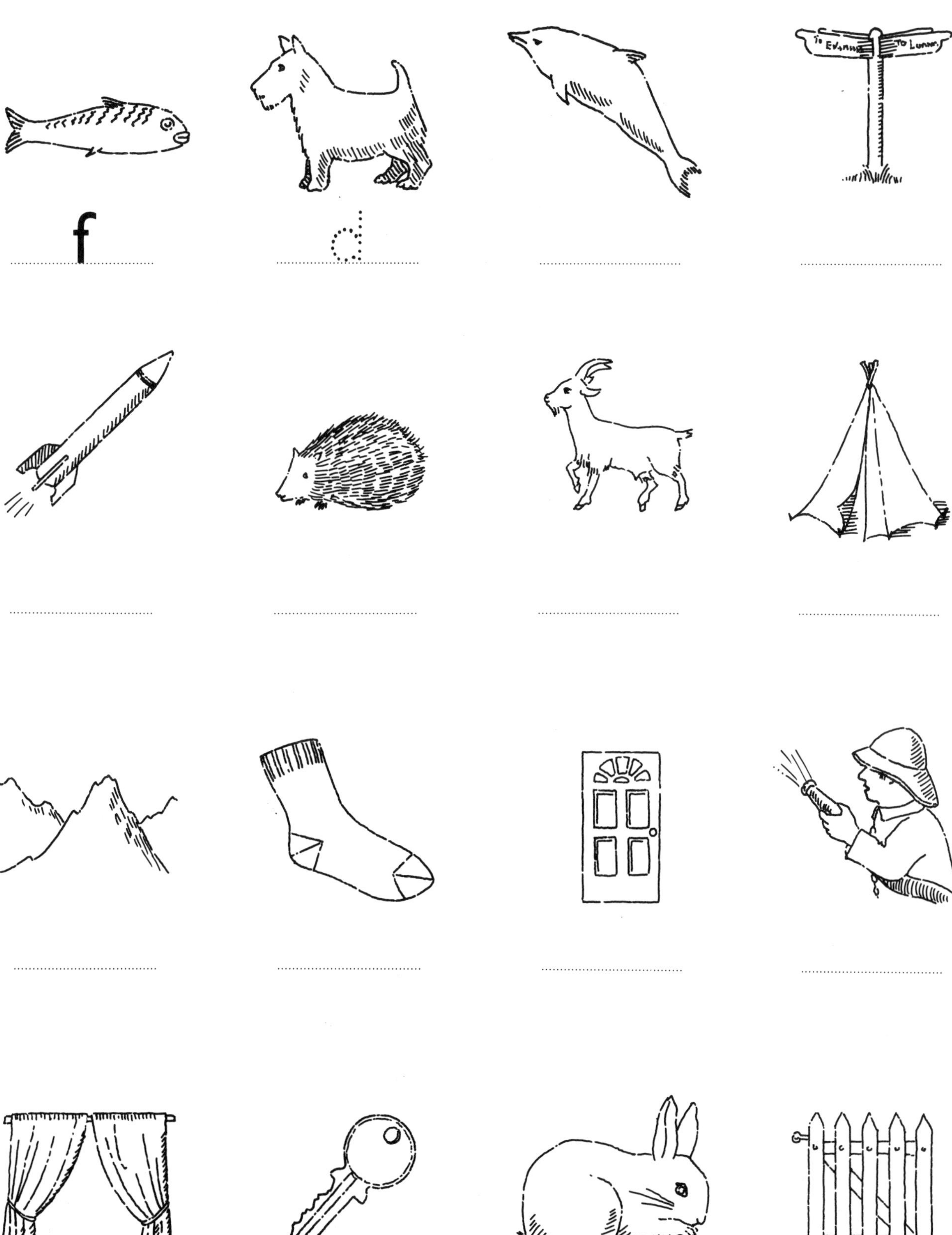
f
d

C.10

Join up the same **last** letters.

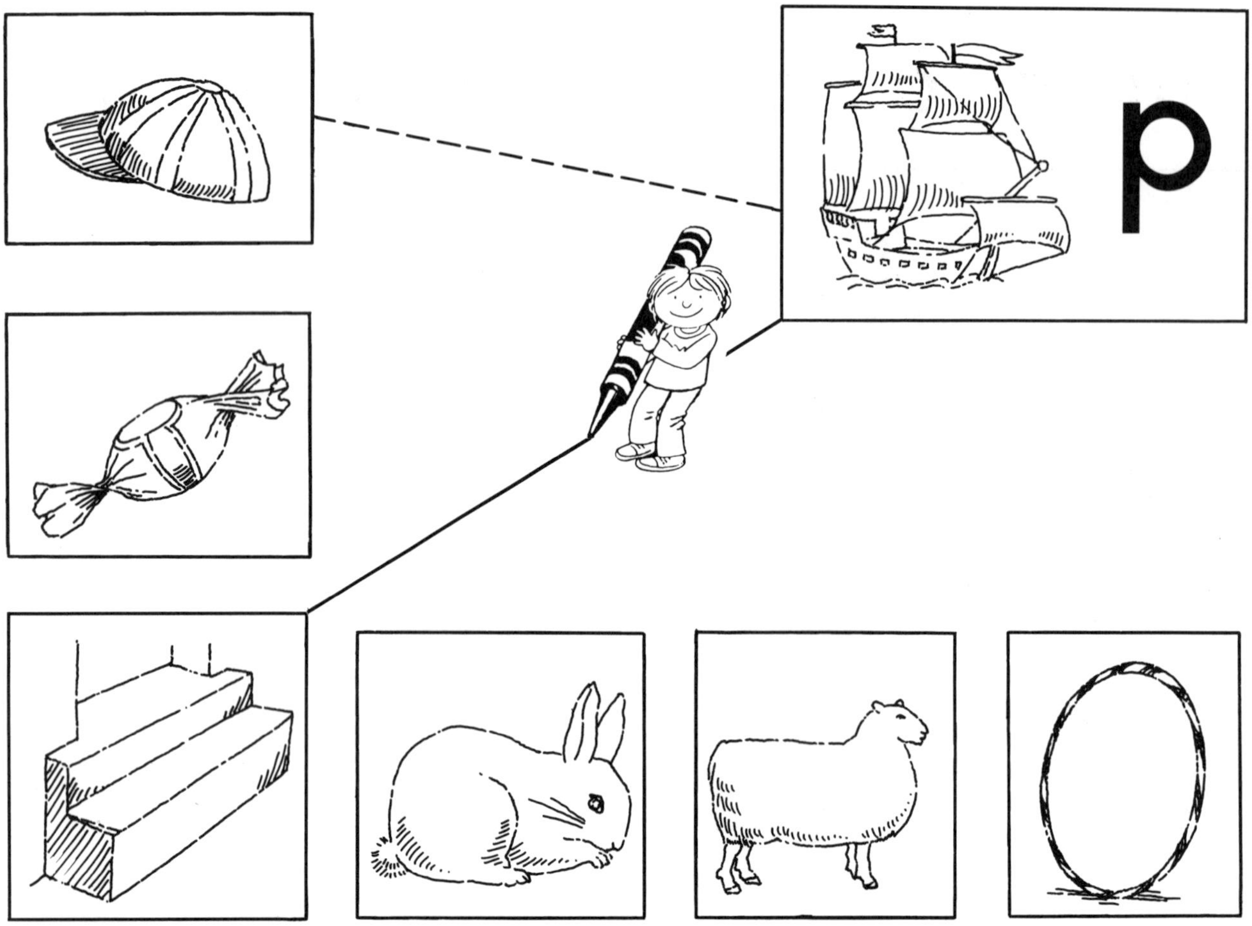

p

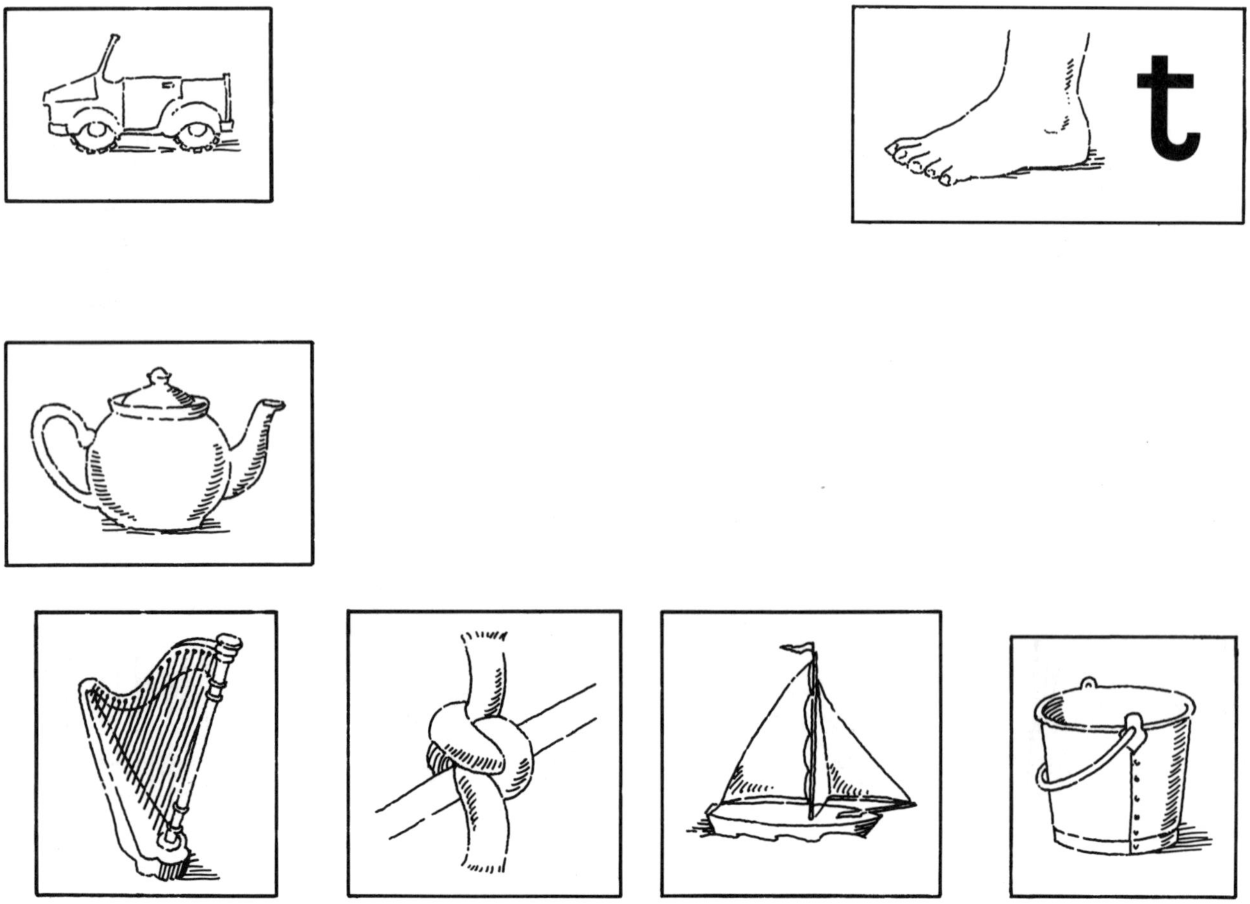

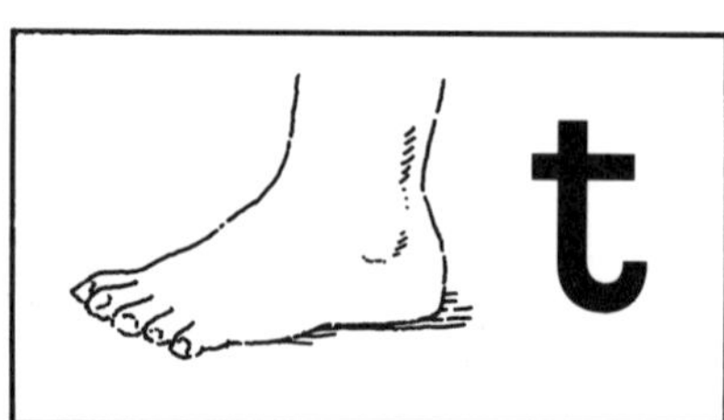
t

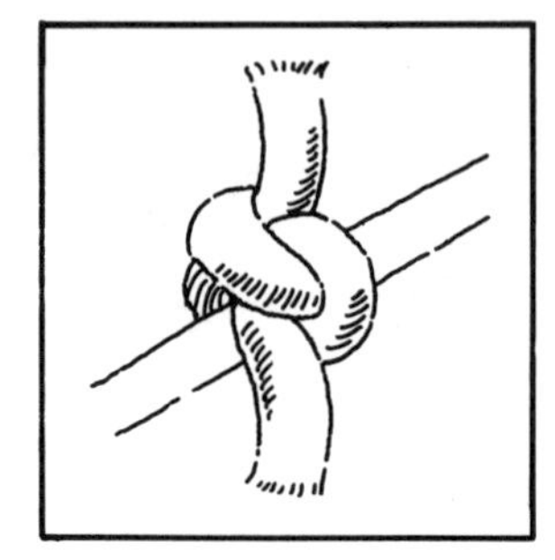

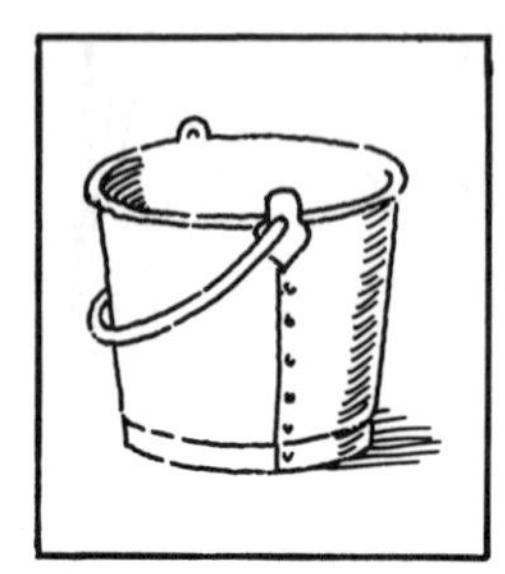

Ring the **first** letter.

d	k	f	s	qu	v	z	y

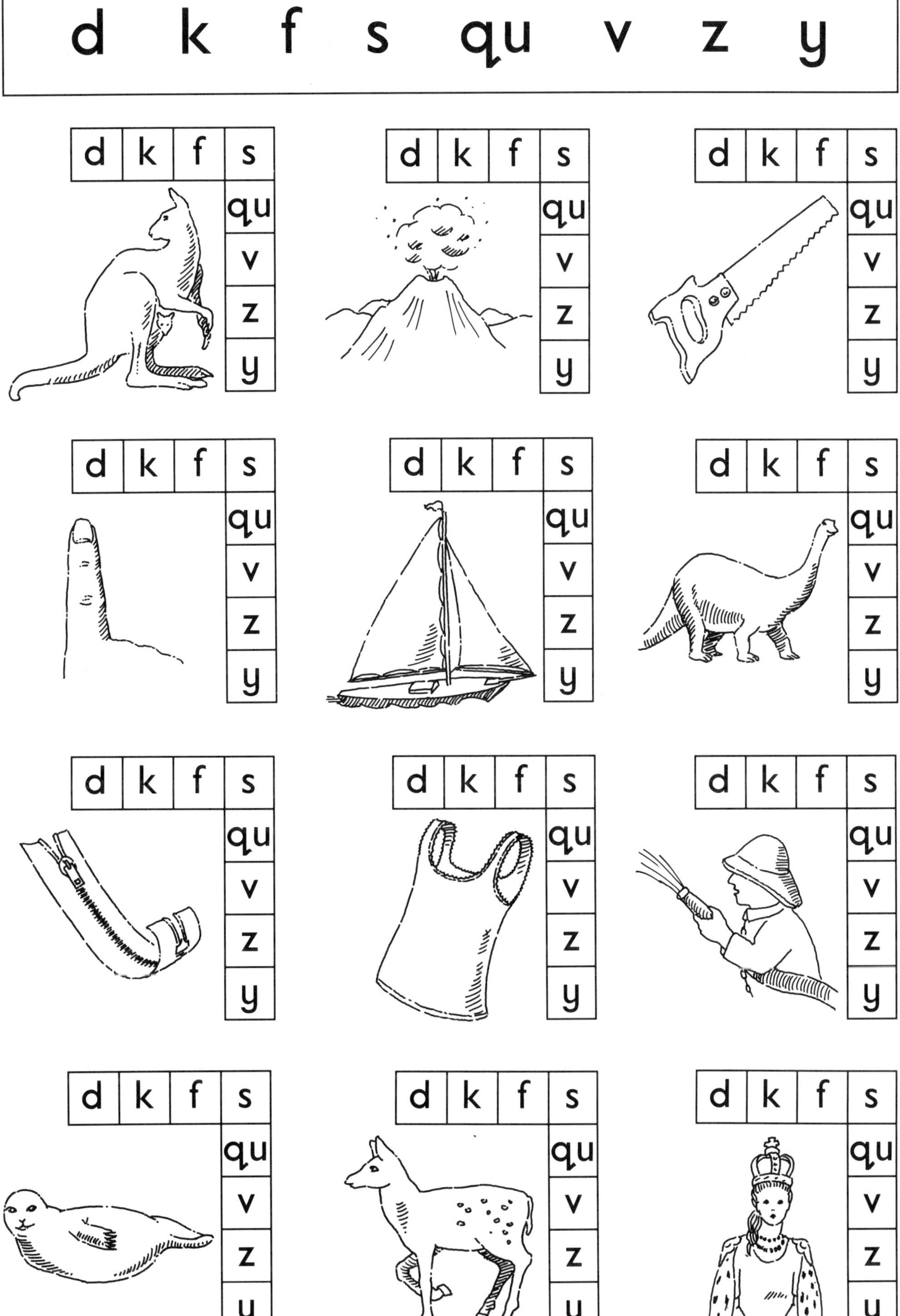
d k f s qu v z y
d k f s qu v z y
d k f s qu v z y
d k f s qu v z y
d k f s qu v z y
d k f s qu v z y
d k f s qu v z y
d k f s qu v z y
d k f s qu v z y
d k f s qu v z y
d k f s qu v z y
d k f s qu v z y

C.12

Put in the **first** letter.

m	c	g	d	k	j	qu	v	z	y

 ....

 ....

 ....

 ....

 ....

 ....

 ....

 ....

 ....

 ....

 ....

 ....

 ....

 ....

 ....

 ....

Join up the same **last** letters.

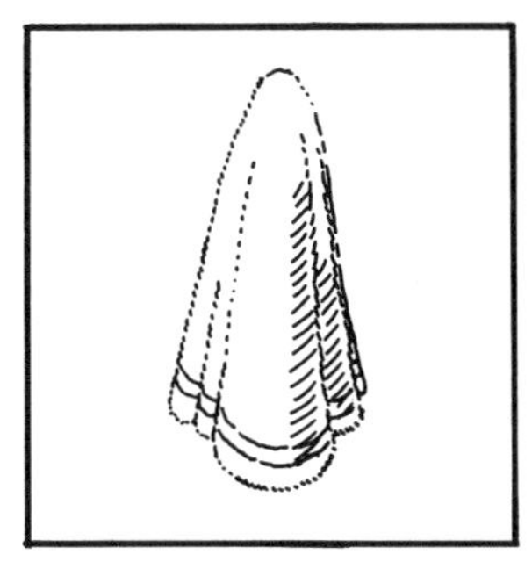

l

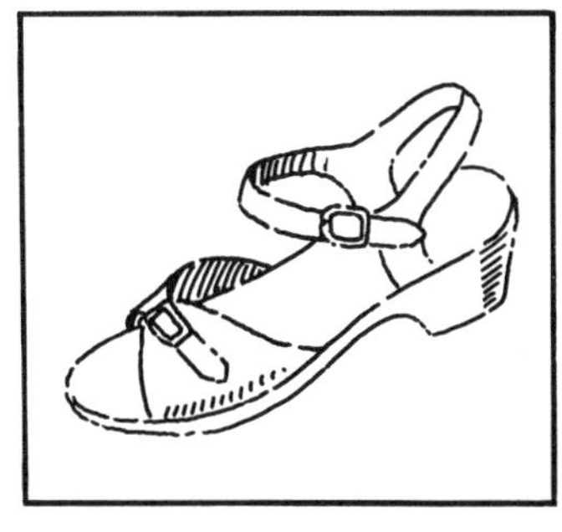
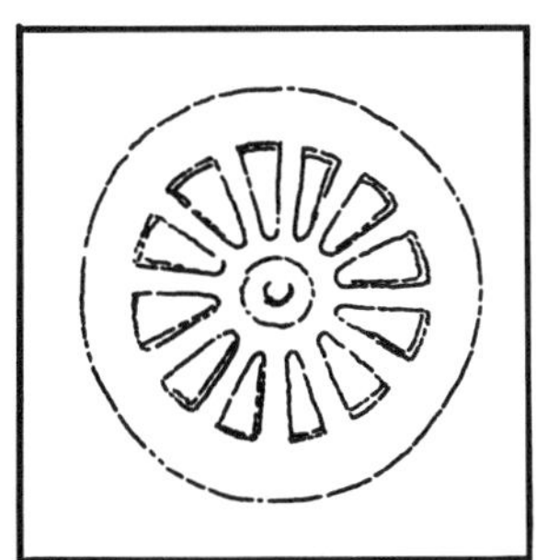
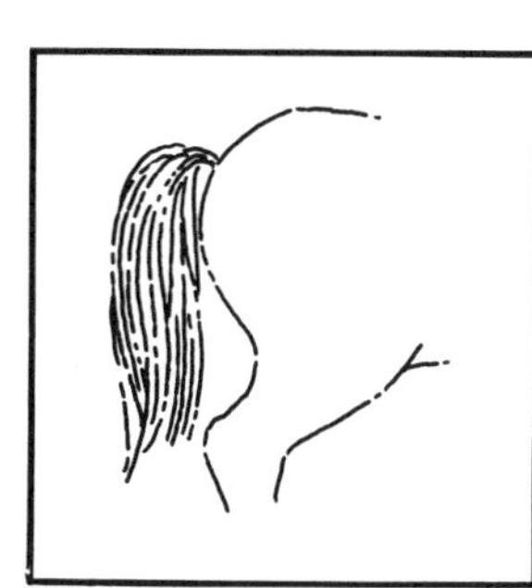
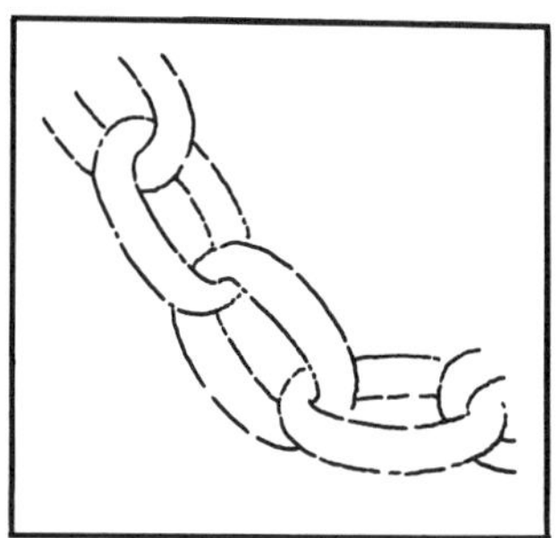

n

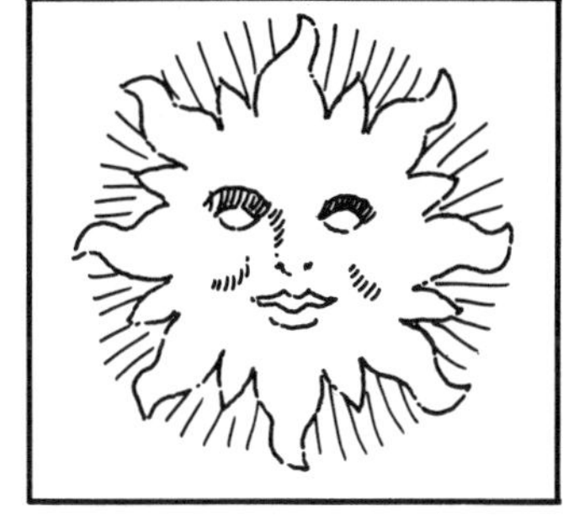

Ring the **first** letter.

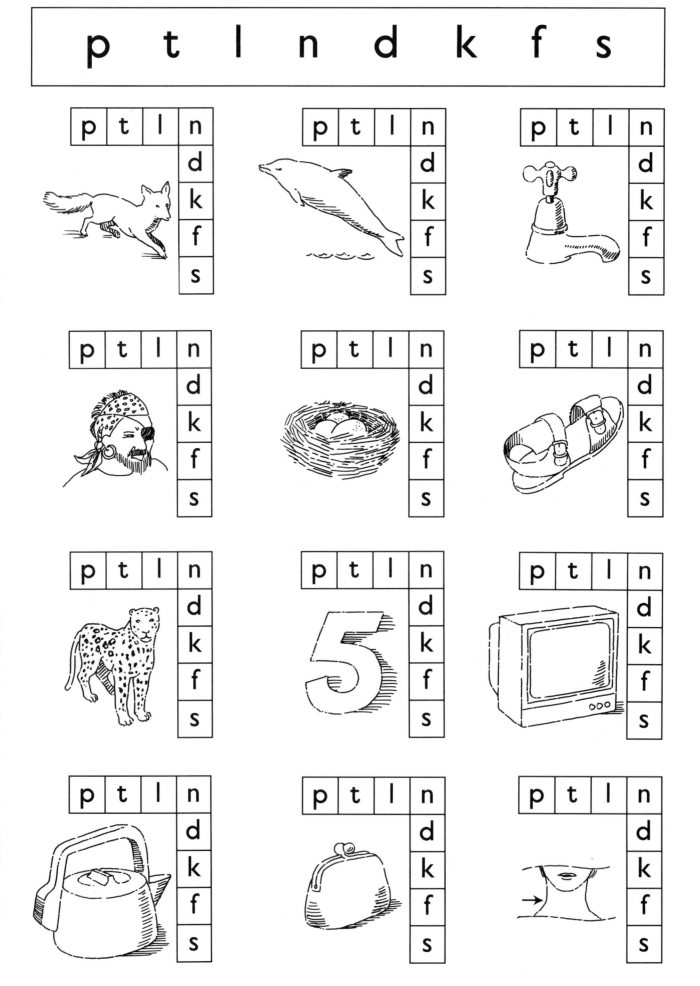

p t l n d k f s

p t l n d k f s

p t l n d k f s

p t l n d k f s

p t l n d k f s

p t l n d k f s

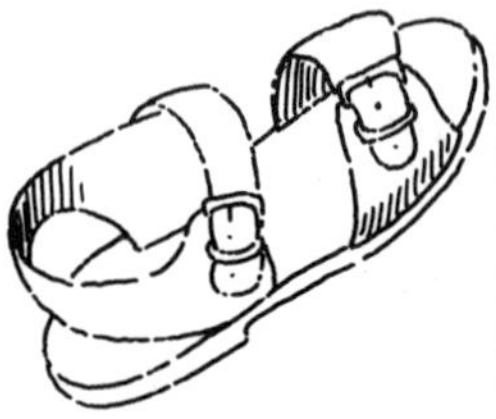

p t l n d k f s

p t l n d k f s

p t l n d k f s

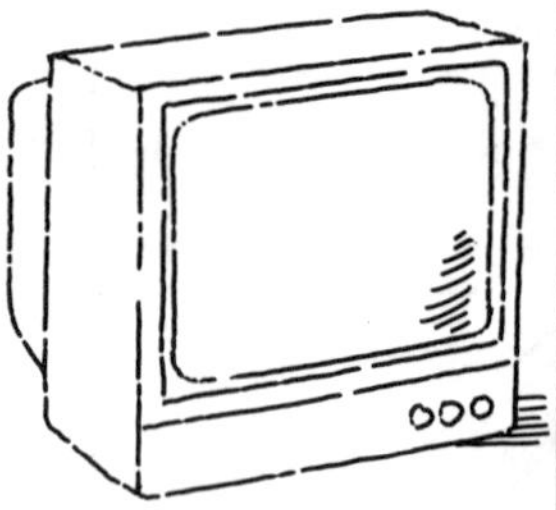

p t l n d k f s

p t l n d k f s

p t l n d k f s

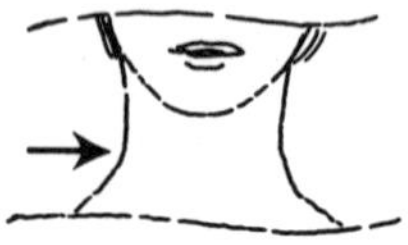

p t l n d k f s

Put in the **first** letter.

f	s	r	h	w	j	qu	v	z	y

 ....

 ....

 ....

 ....

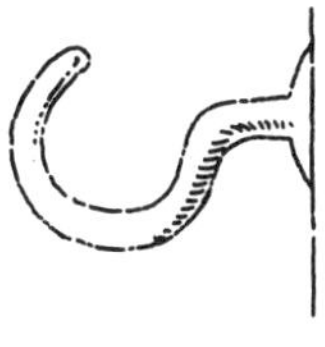 ....

 ....

 ....

 ....

 ....

 ....

 ....

 ....

 ....

 ....

 ....

 ....

C.16

Join up the same **last** letters.

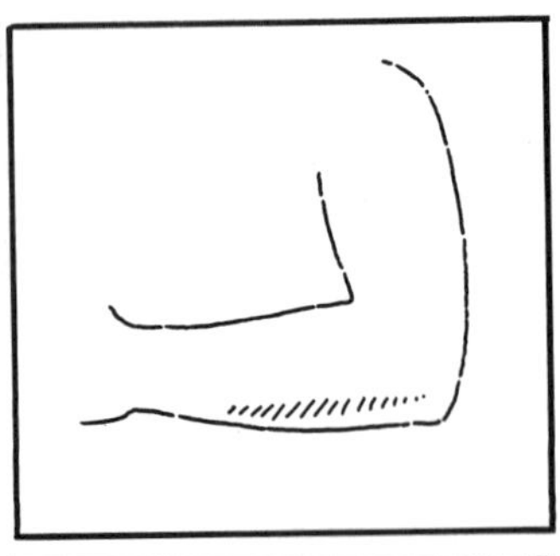

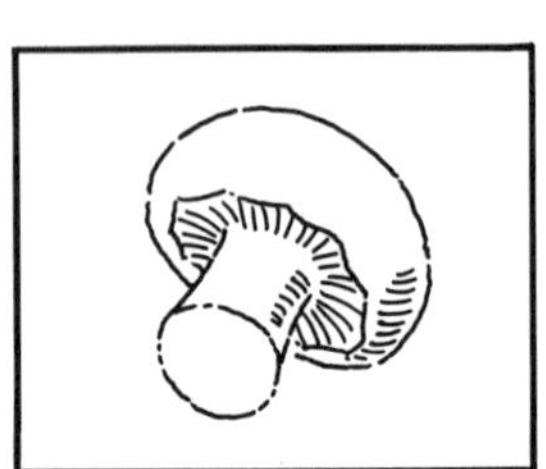

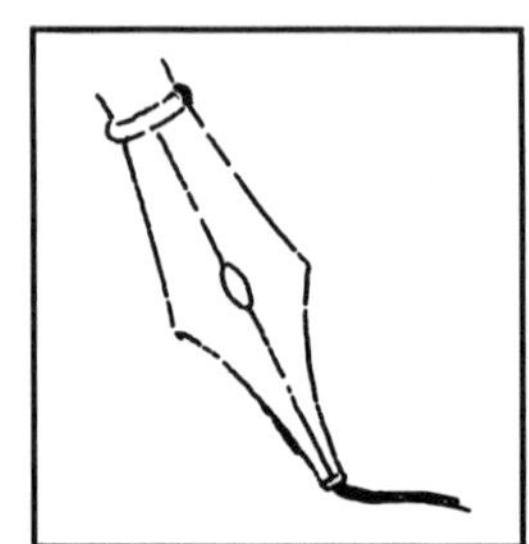

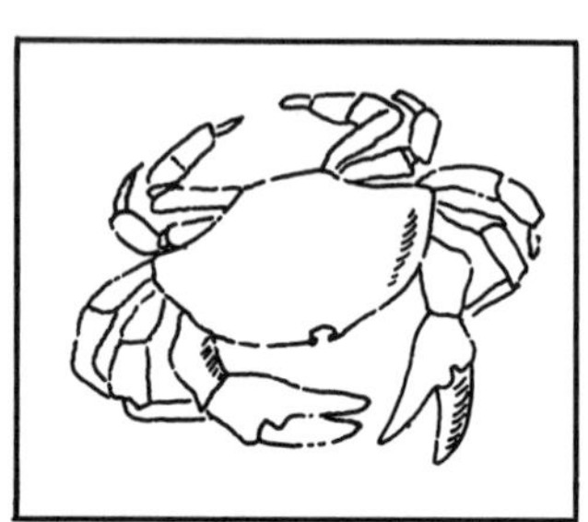

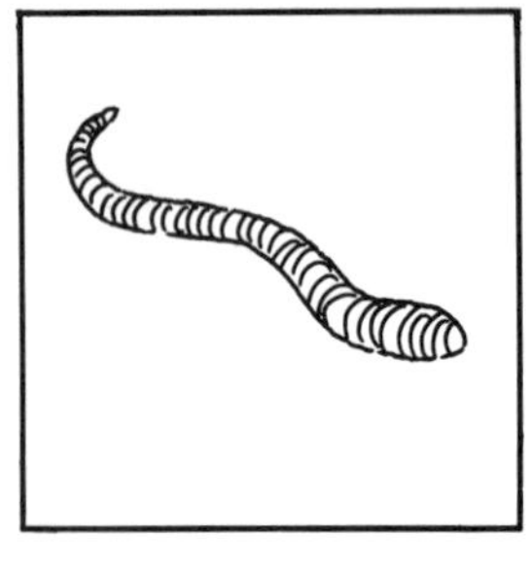

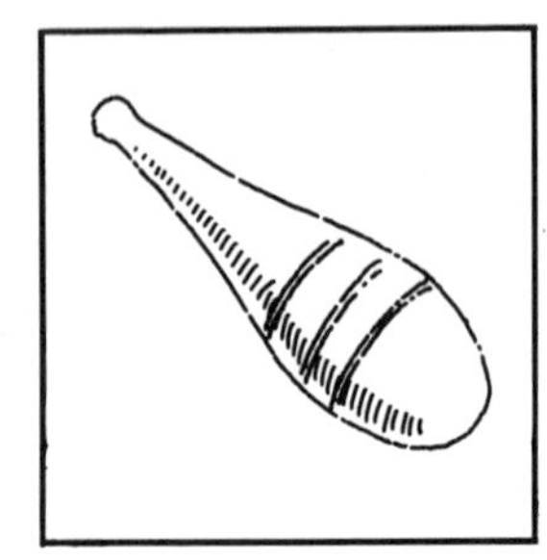

Ring the **first** letter.

p t l n r w h j

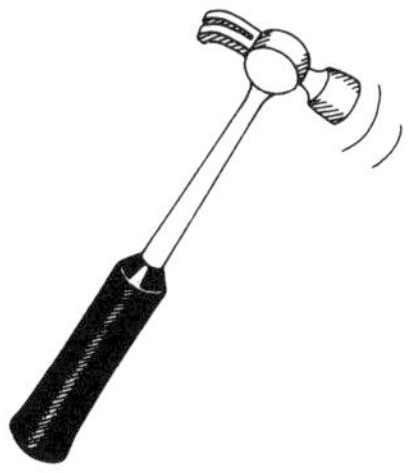

p t l n r w h j

p t l n r w h j

p t l n r w h j

p t l n r w h j

p t l n r w h j

p t l n r w h j

p t l n r w h j

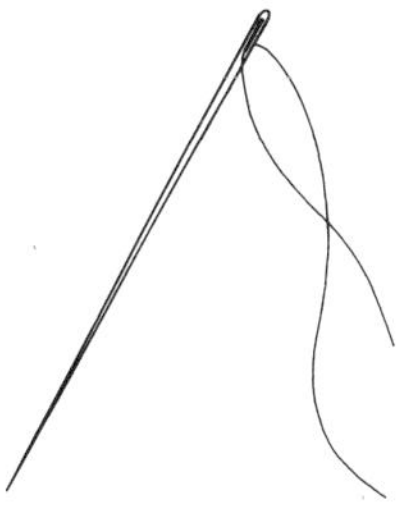

p t l n r w h j

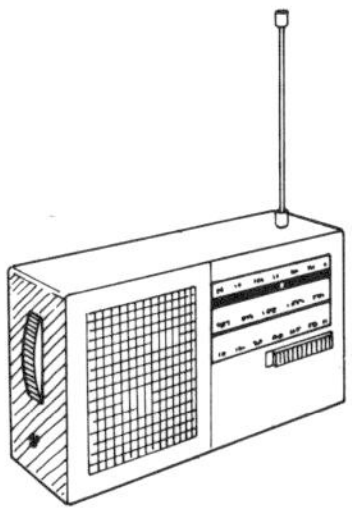

p t l n r w h j

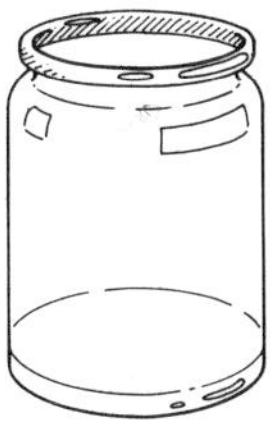

p t l n r w h j

p t l n r w h j

p t l n r w h j

Put in the **first** letter.

p	t	l	n	b	f	s	r	w	h

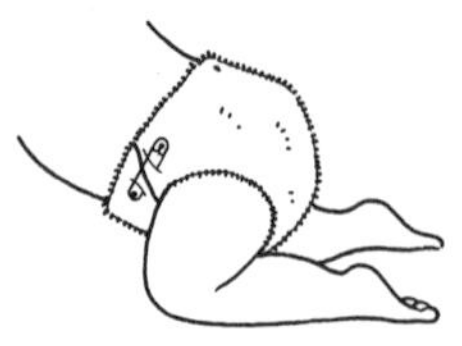

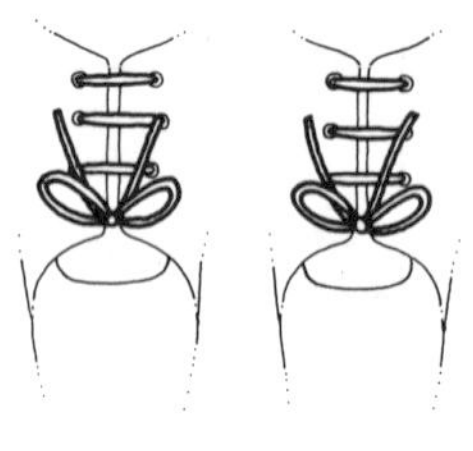
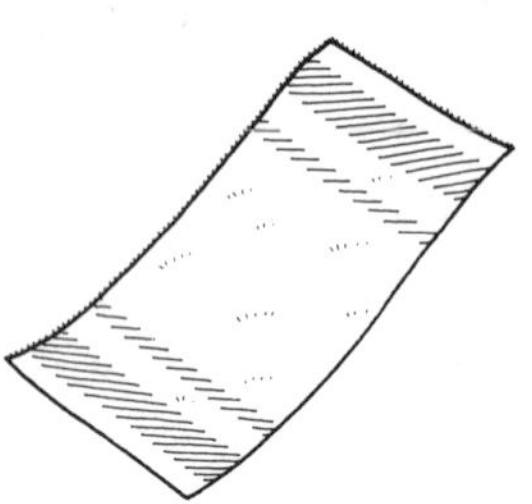
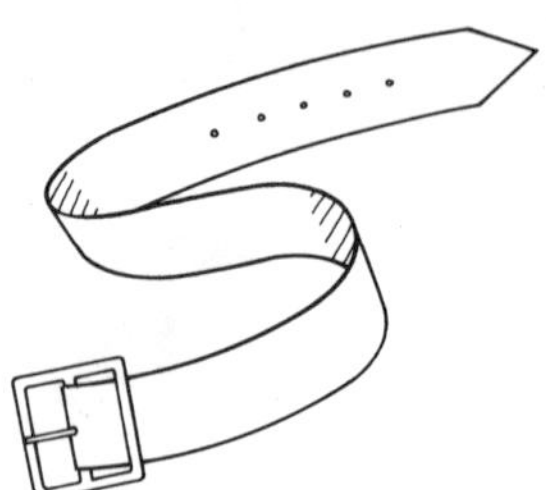

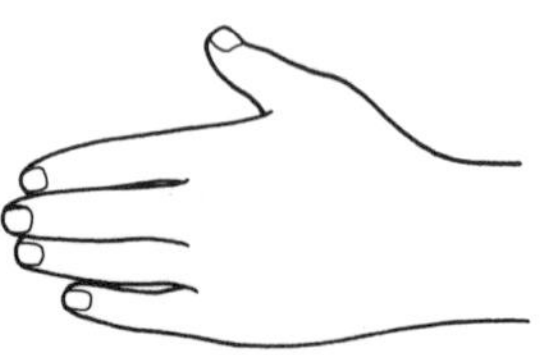
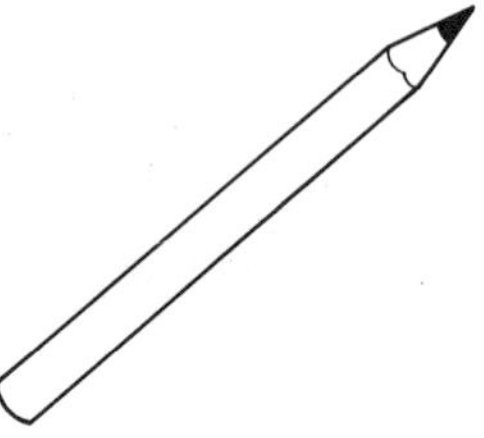

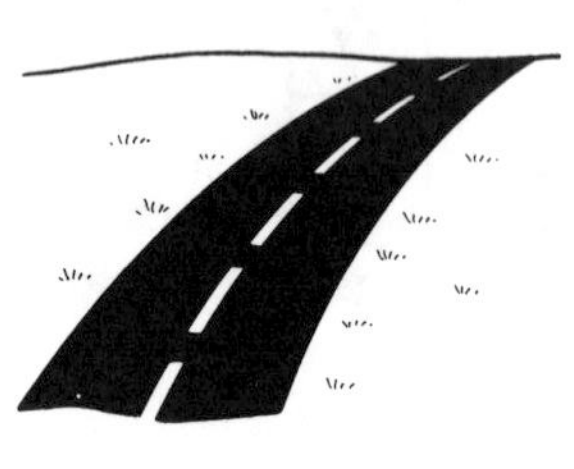
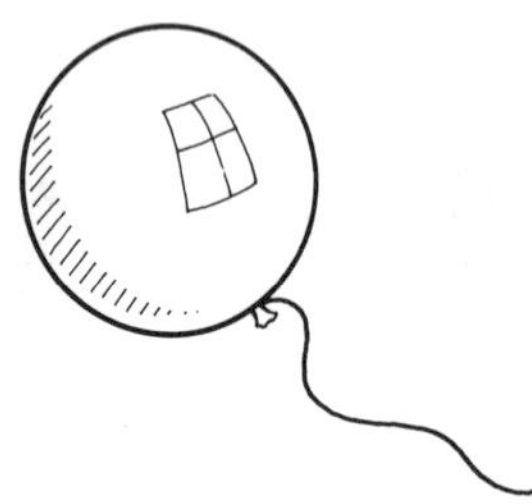

Join up the same **last** letters.

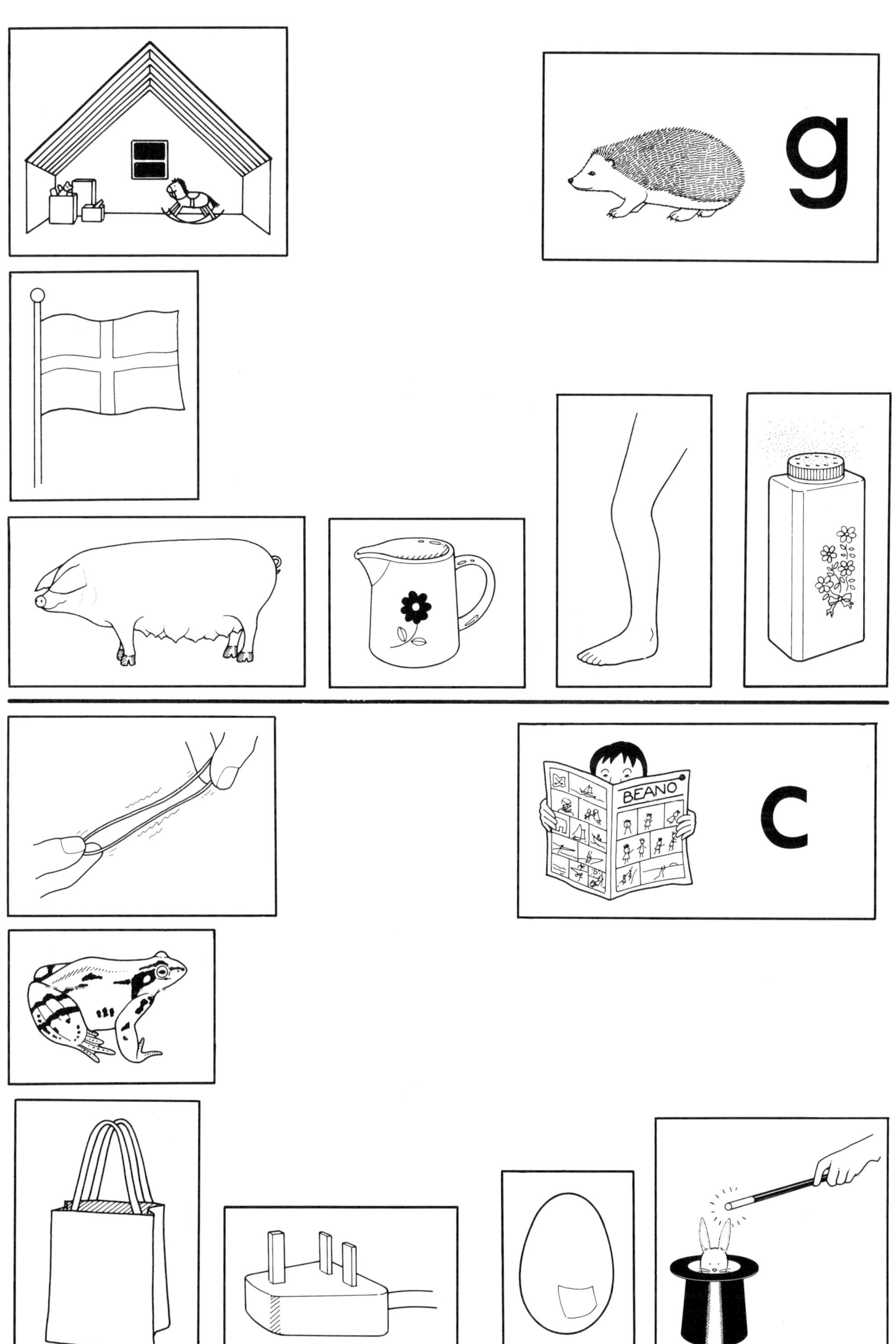
g
BEANO
c

Ring the **first** letter.

b	m	c	g	qu	v	z	y

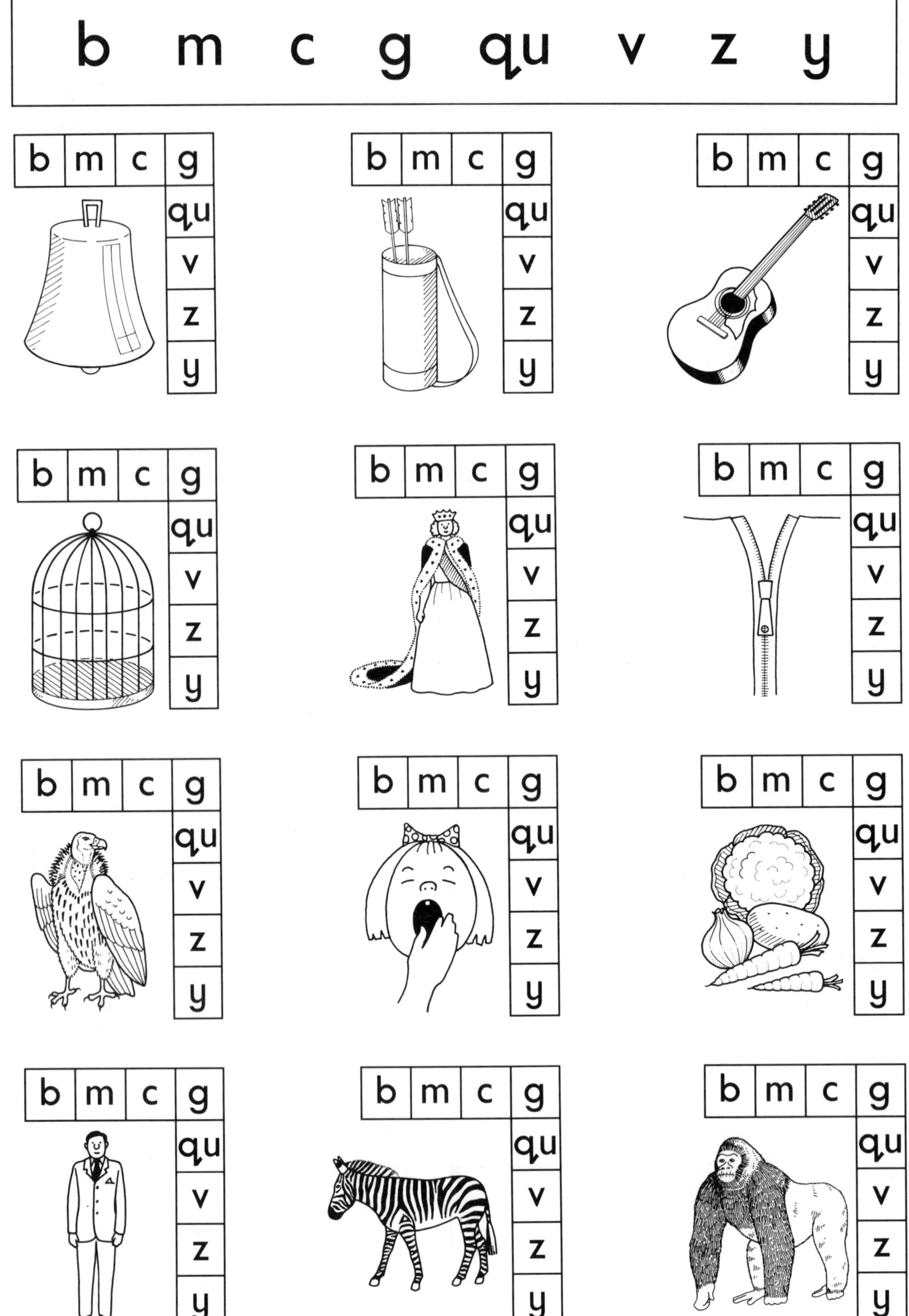
b m c g qu v z y
b m c g qu v z y
b m c g qu v z y
b m c g qu v z y
b m c g qu v z y
b m c g qu v z y
b m c g qu v z y
b m c g qu v z y
b m c g qu v z y
b m c g qu v z y
b m c g qu v z y
b m c g qu v z y

Put in the **first** letter.

p t l n b j qu v z y

....
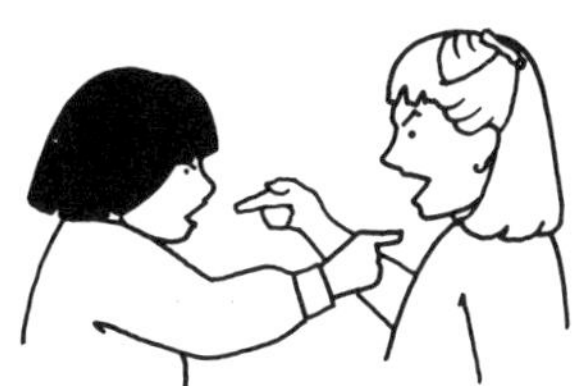
....

....
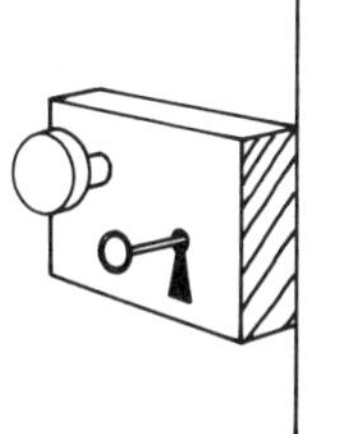
....

....
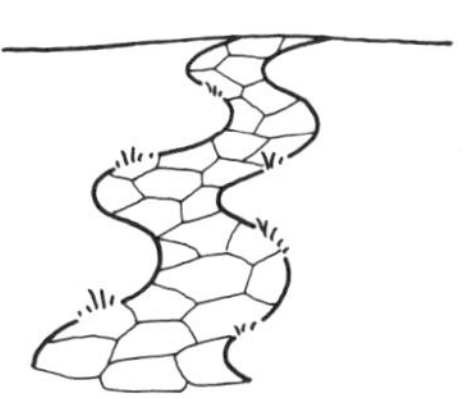
....

....
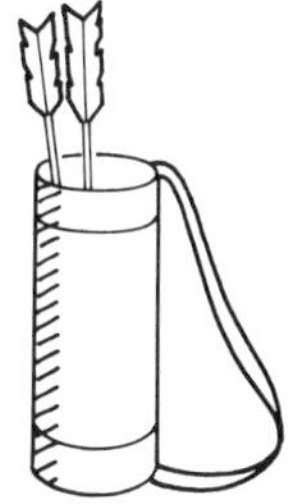
....

....

....

....

....

....

....
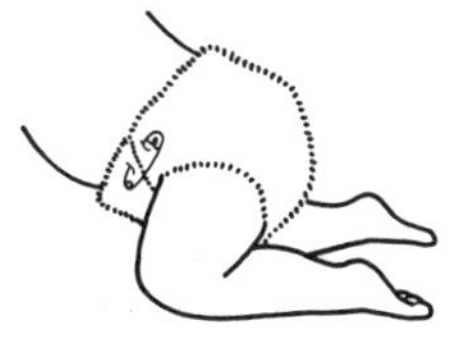
....
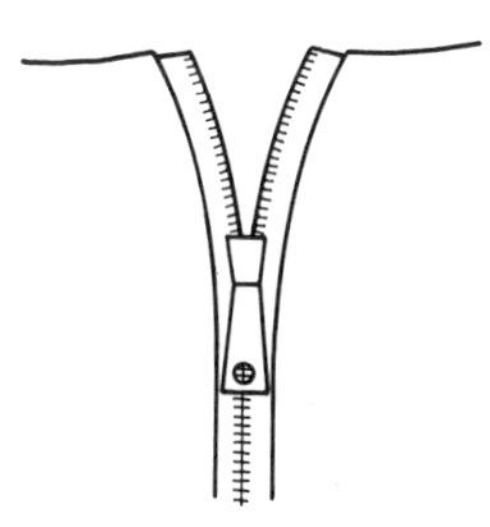
....

D.6

Join up the same **last** letters.

d

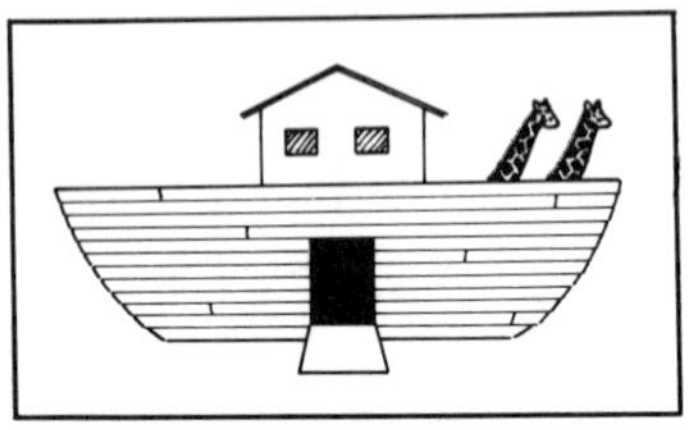

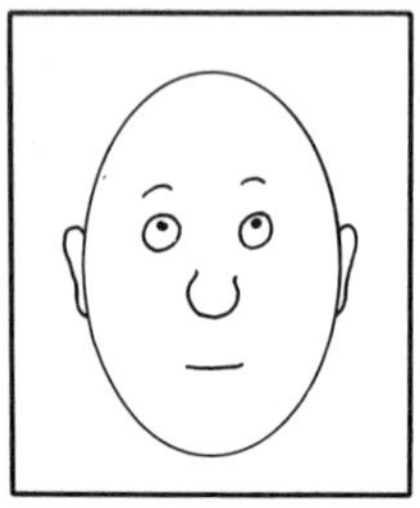

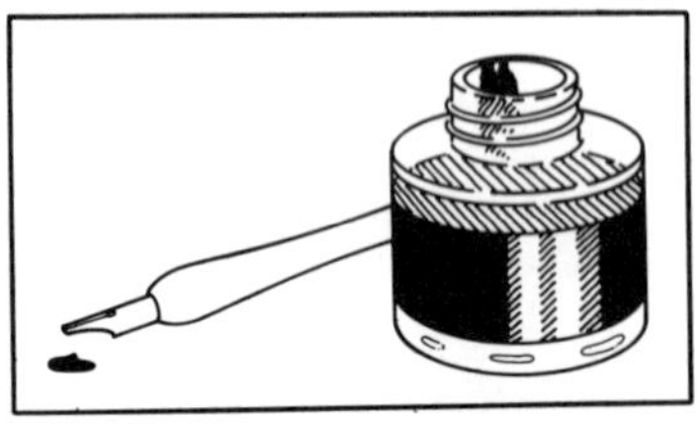

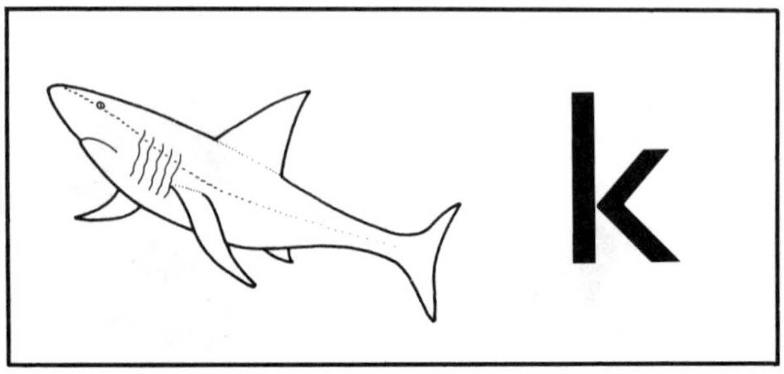

k

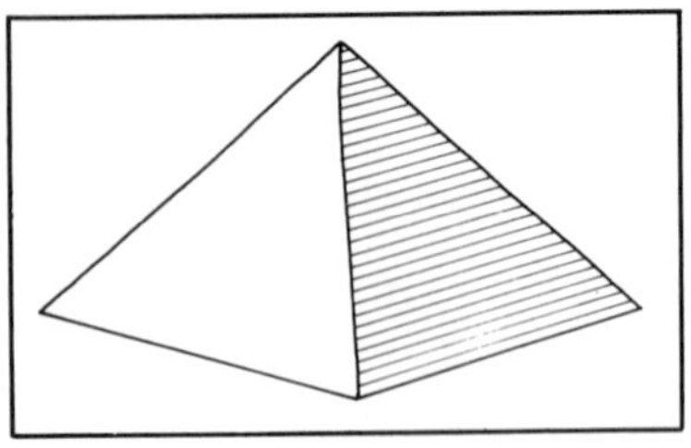

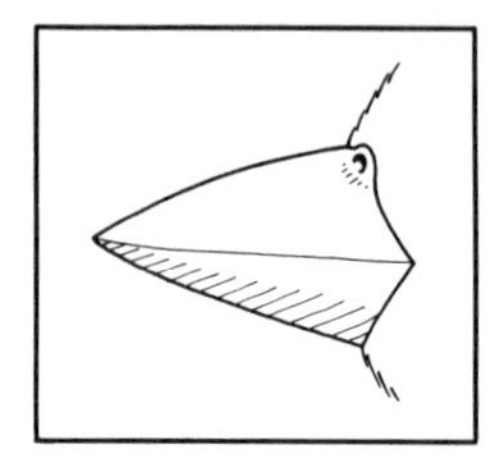

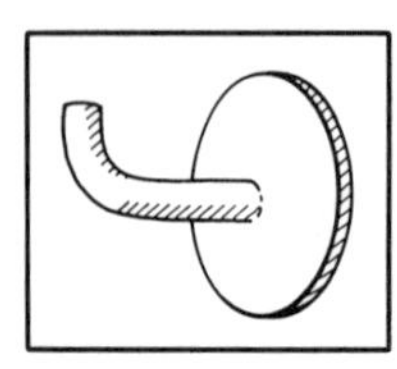

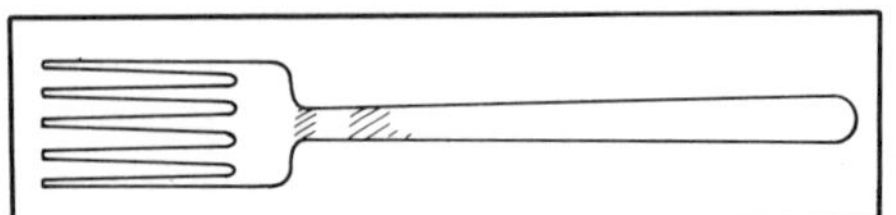

Ring the **first** letter.

r w h j qu v z y

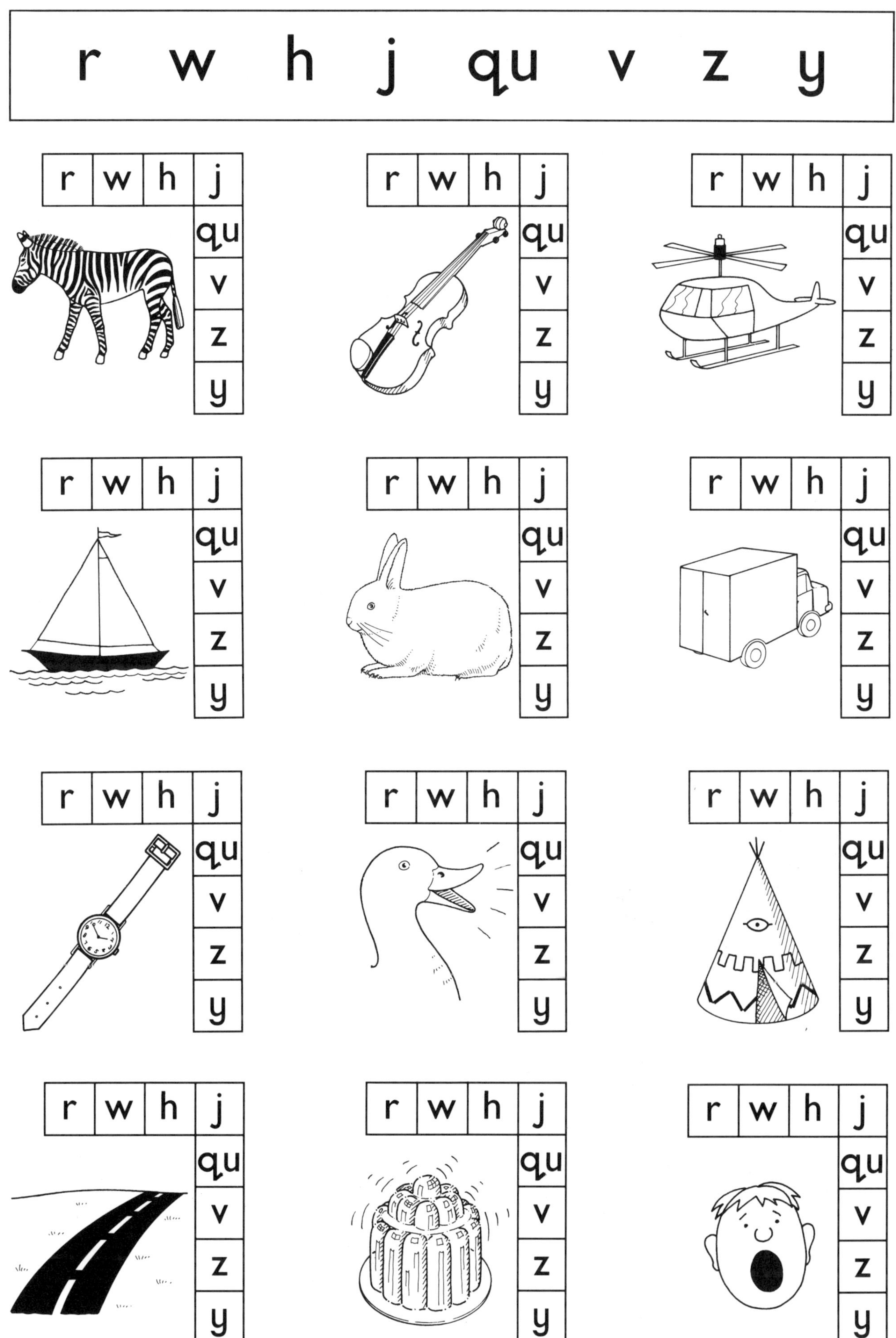
r w h j qu v z y
r w h j qu v z y
r w h j qu v z y
r w h j qu v z y
r w h j qu v z y
r w h j qu v z y
r w h j qu v z y
r w h j qu v z y
r w h j qu v z y
r w h j qu v z y
r w h j qu v z y
r w h j qu v z y

D.8

Put in the **first** letter.

p	t	l	n	b	m	c	g	d	k

   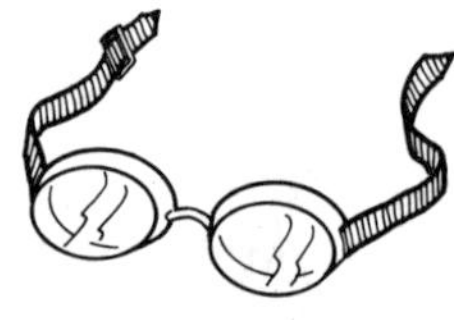

q  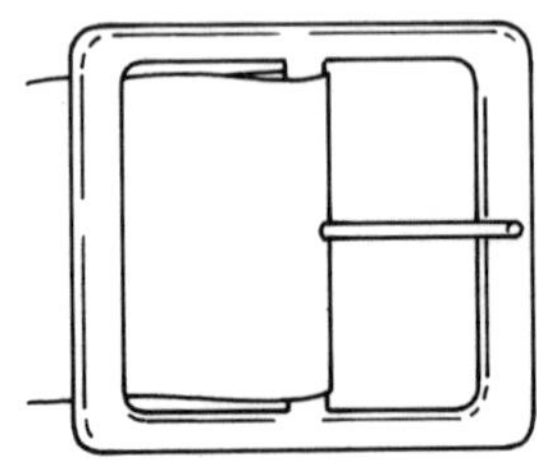 

 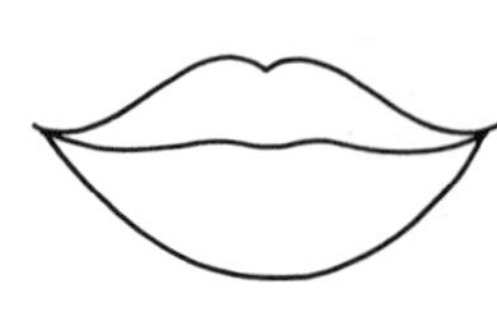  

Join up the same **last** letters.

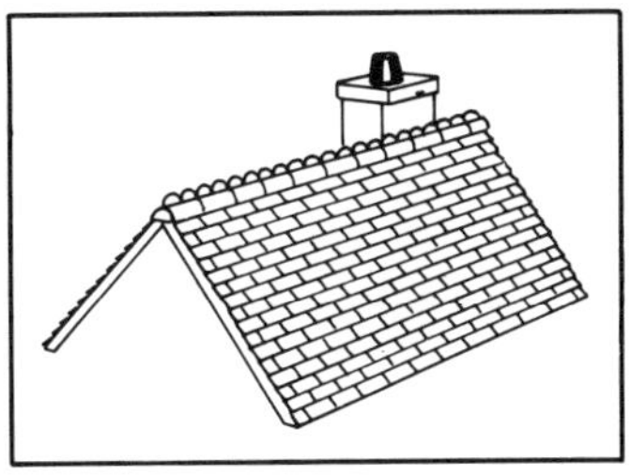

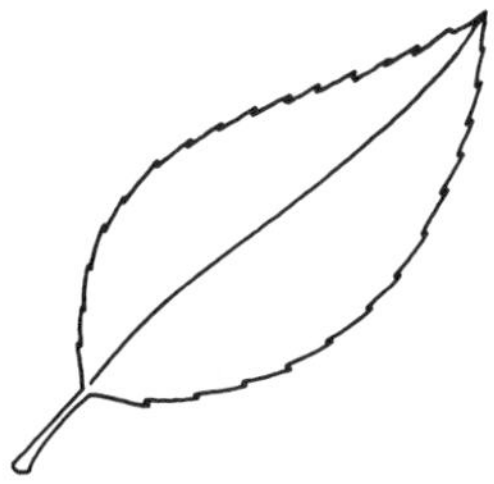

f

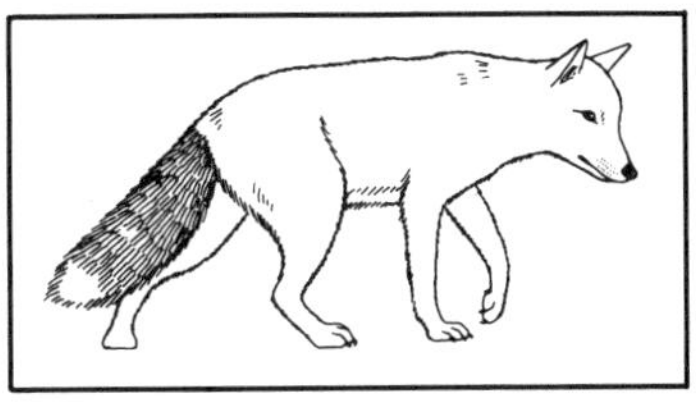

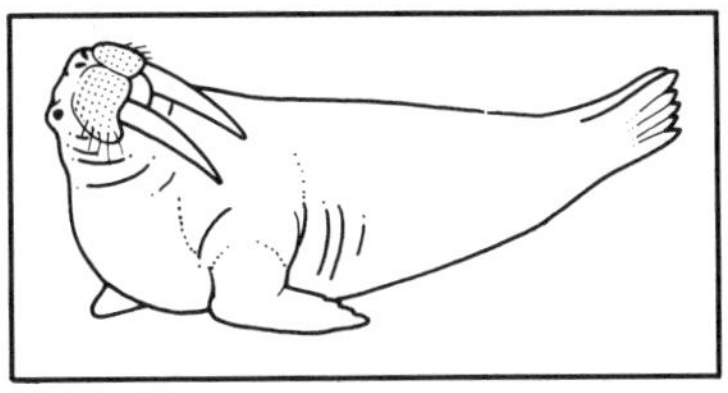

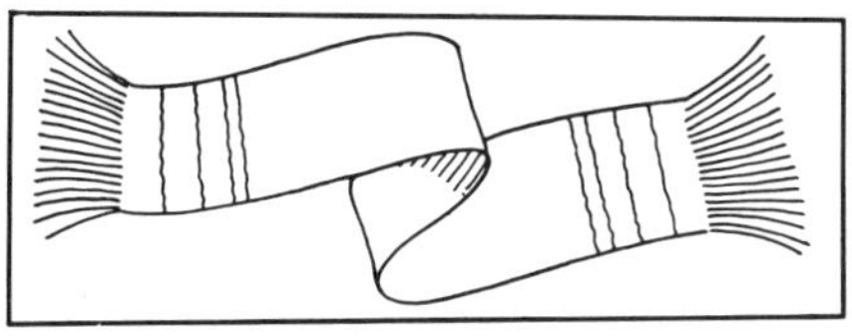

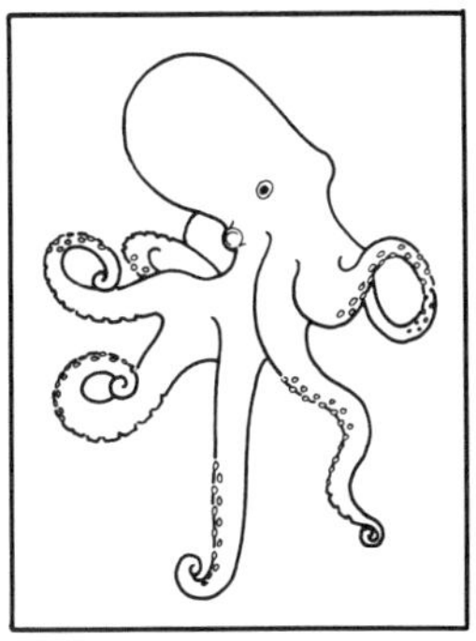

s

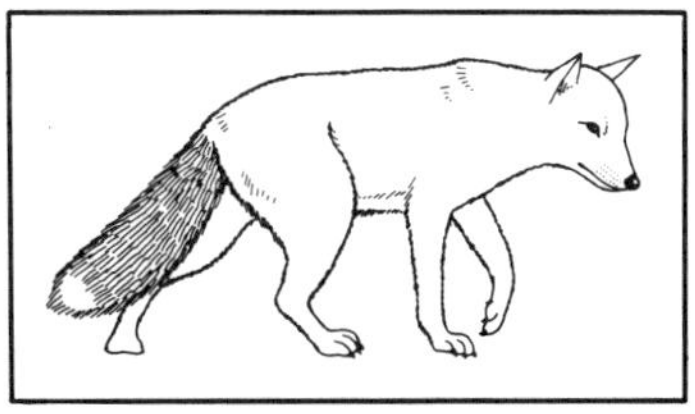

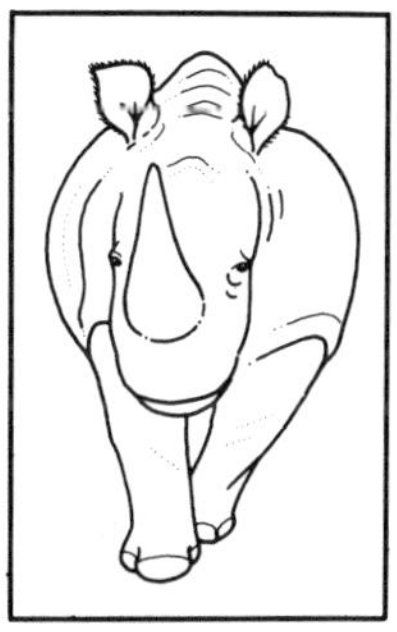

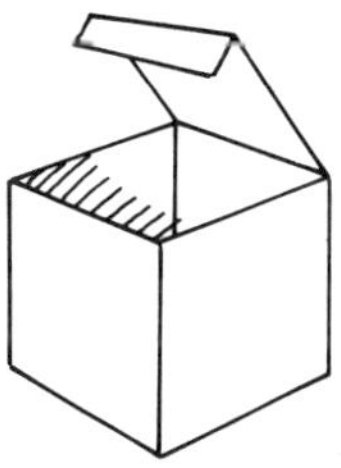

x

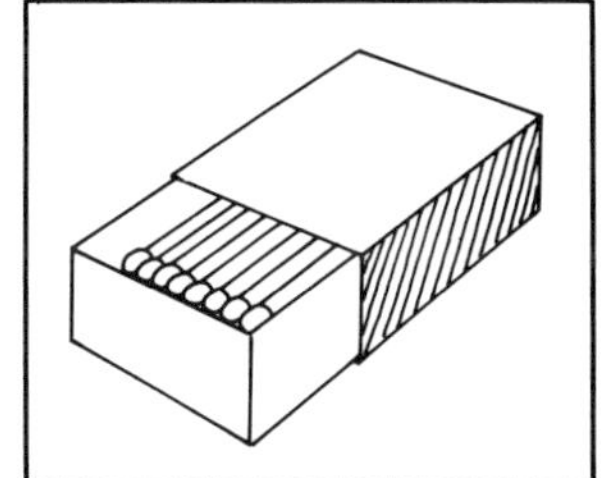

6

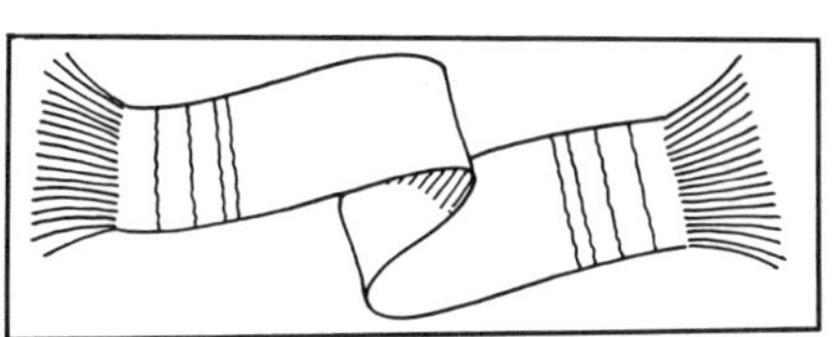

Ring the **first** letter.

b	m	g	c	d	k	f	s

b m g c
d
k
f
s

b m g c
d
k
f
s

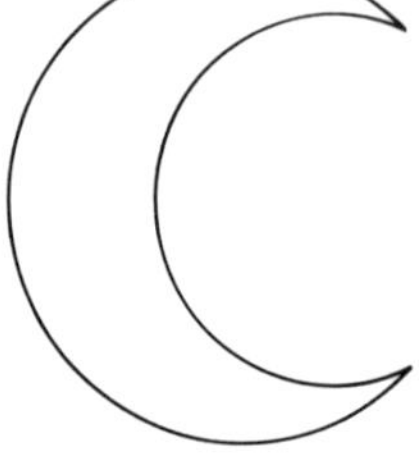

b m g c
d
k
f
s

b m g c
d
k
f
s

b m g c
d
k
f
s

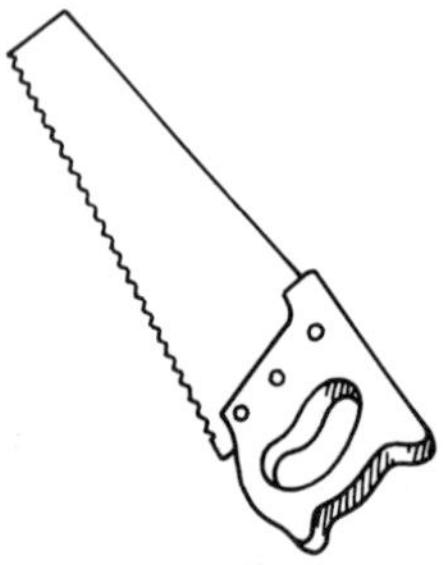

b m g c
d
k
f
s

b m g c
d
k
f
s

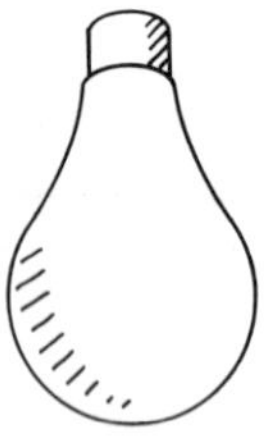

b m g c
d
k
f
s

b m g c
d
k
f
s

b m g c
d
k
f
s

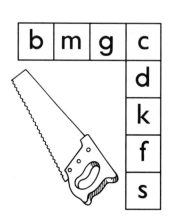

b m g c
d
k
f
s

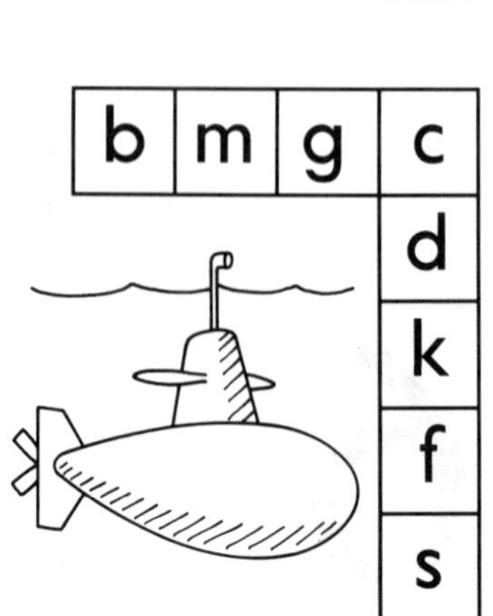

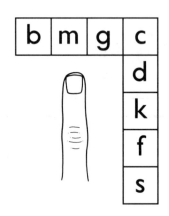

b m g c
d
k
f
s

Put in the words.

b f s
l qu h p
it

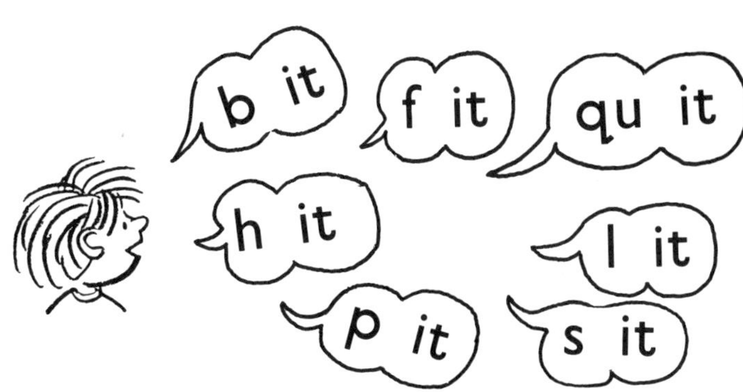
b it
f it
qu it
h it
l it
p it
s it

bit	hit	pit
bit	hit	pit
b	h	p

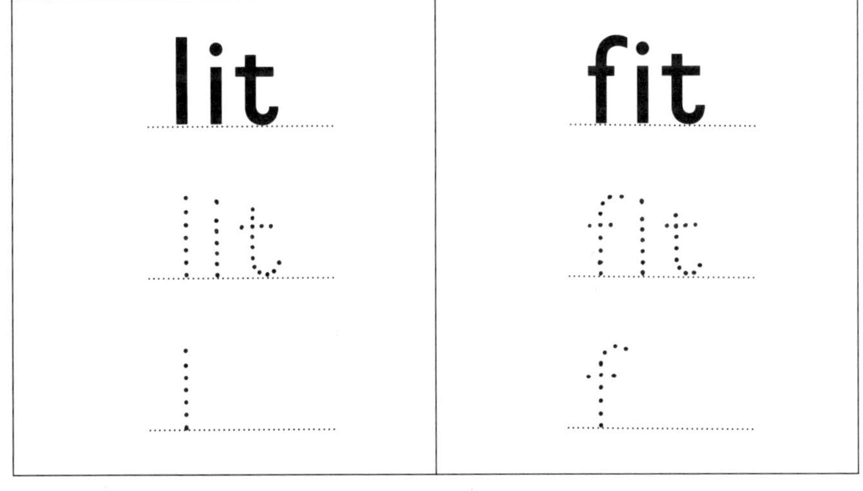
lit
lit
l
fit
fit
f

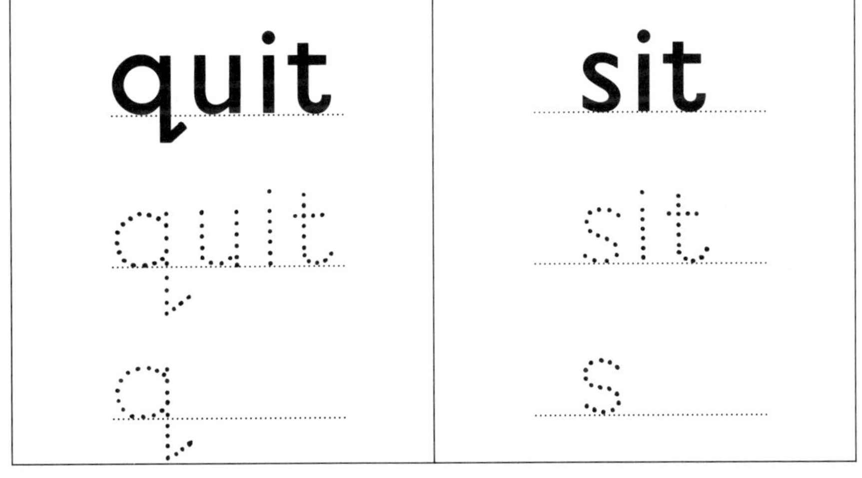
quit
quit
q
sit
sit
s

Put in the words.

d t b f p
w
in

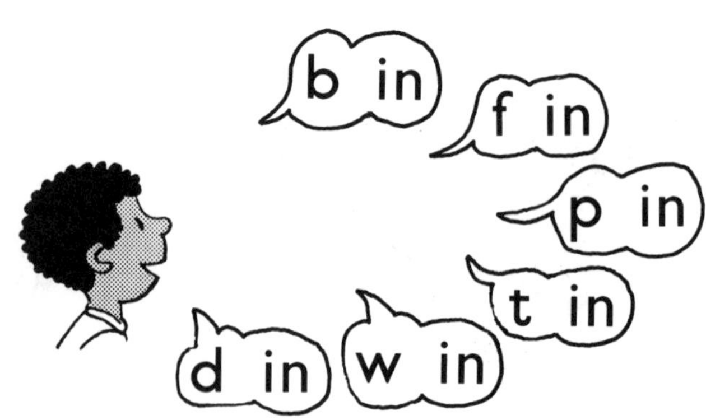
b in
f in
p in
t in
d in
w in

fin	tin	din	win
fin	tin	din	win
f	t	d	w

Put it in the bin.	Wilma looked at the ________.	Dad gave Mum a ________.
He wanted to ________.	Who put down a ________?	Stop the ________.

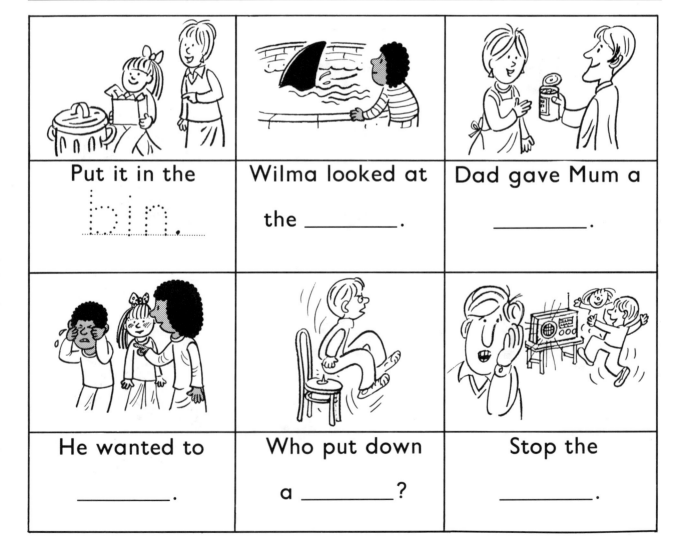

Put in the words.

l b s h
and

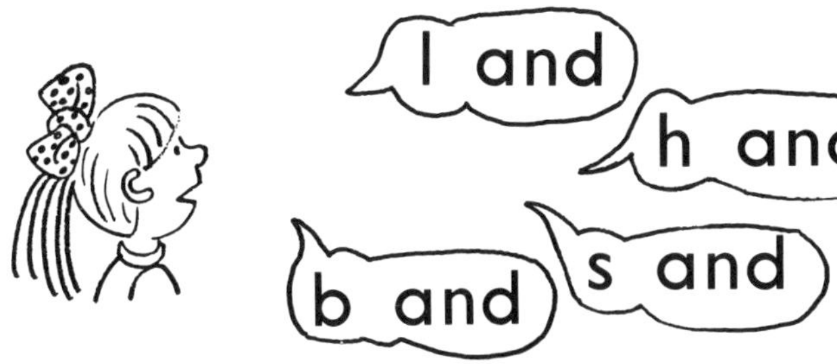
l and
h and
s and
b and

land	hand	sand	band
land	hand	sand	band
l	h	s	b

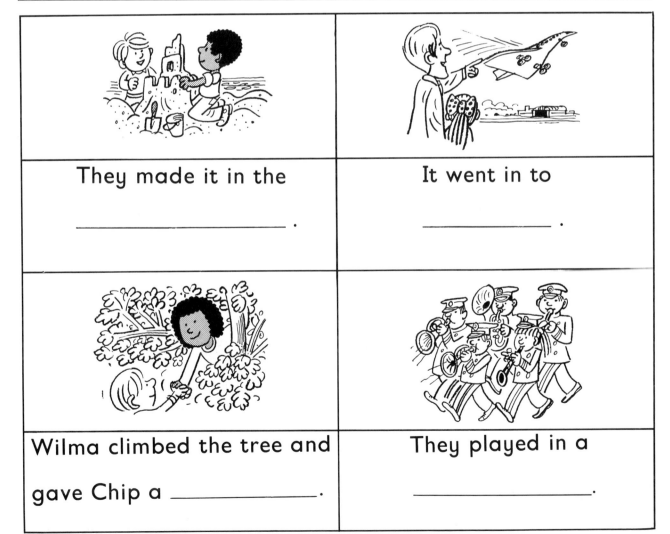

They made it in the ______________.	It went in to ____________.
Wilma climbed the tree and gave Chip a ____________.	They played in a ____________.

D.14

Put in the words.

d h j y r
am

jam
ram
dam
ham
yam

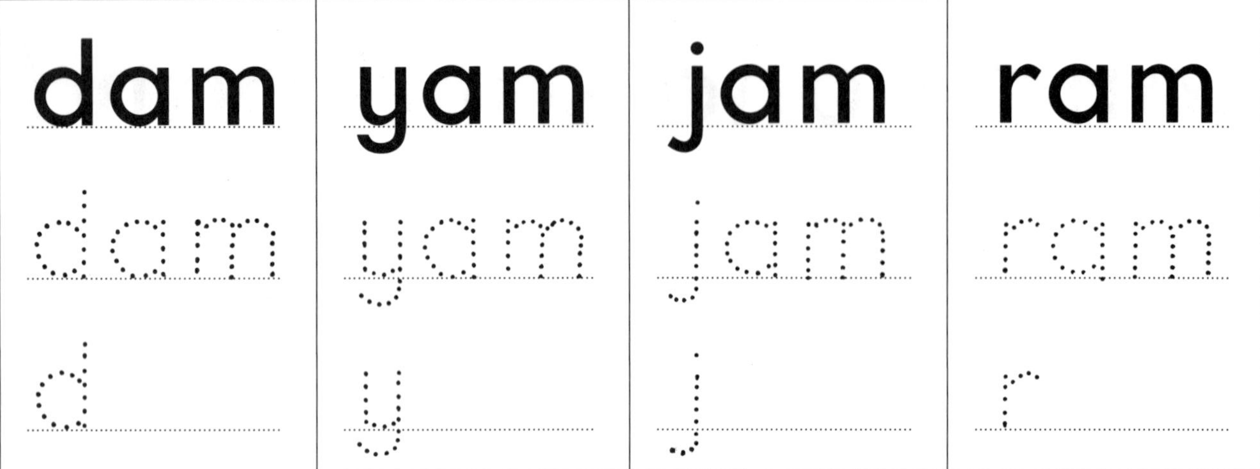

dam
yam
jam
ram
dam
yam
jam
ram
d
y
j
r

Everyone looked at the ______.	Floppy barked at a ______.
Kipper had ______.	Wilma had got a ______.

Put in the words.

c h r s
b f p
at

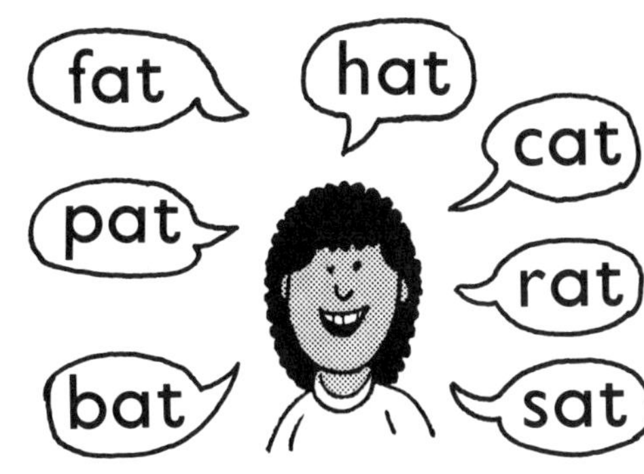
fat
hat
cat
pat
rat
bat
sat

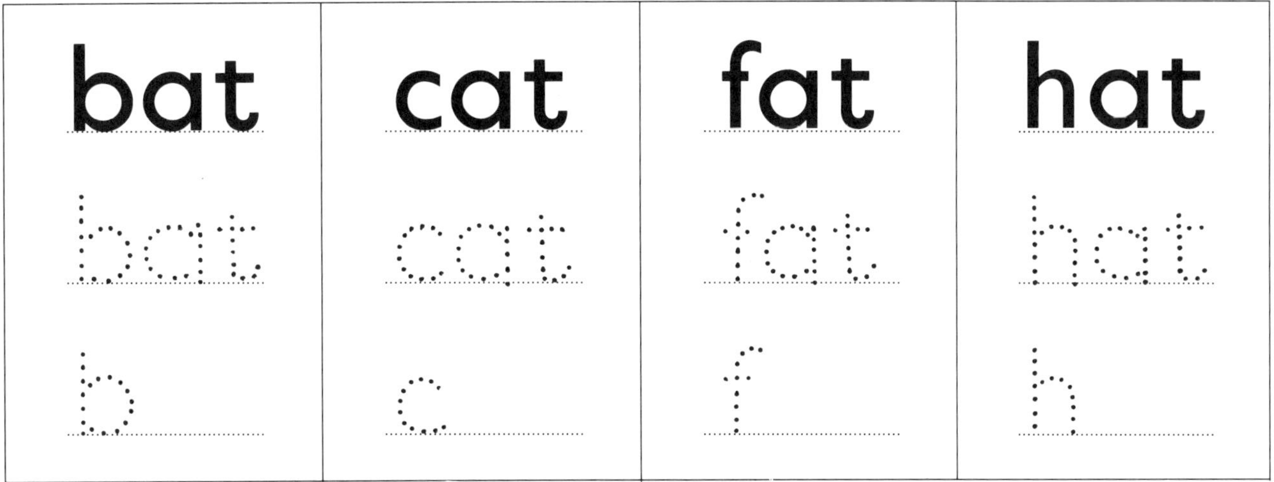
bat
cat
fat
hat
bat
cat
fat
hat
b
c
f
h

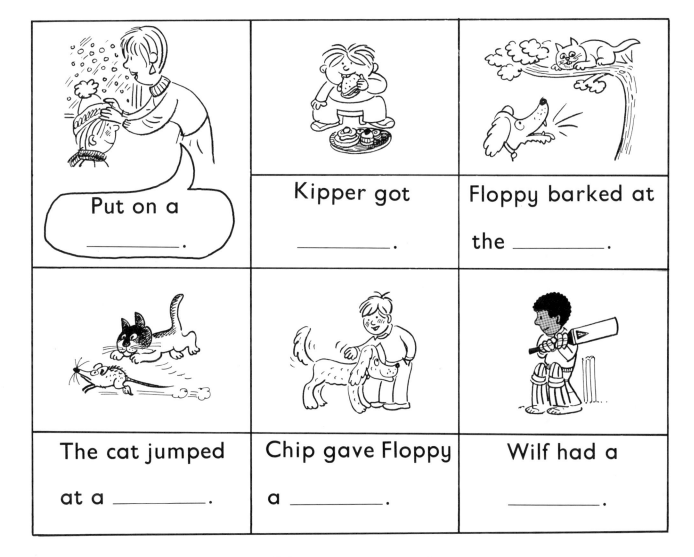

Put on a ________.	Kipper got ________.	Floppy barked at the ________.
The cat jumped at a ________.	Chip gave Floppy a ________.	Wilf had a ________.

Capital letters

Put in the capital letters.

c C	o	p	s
u	v	w	x
z	i	k	m
f	l	j	y
n	h	b	t
d	q	r	g
a	e		

A	B	C	D	E	F	G	H
I	J	K	L	M	N	O	P
Q	R	S	T	U	V	W	X
Y	Z						

Saw and draw with the Word Wizard.

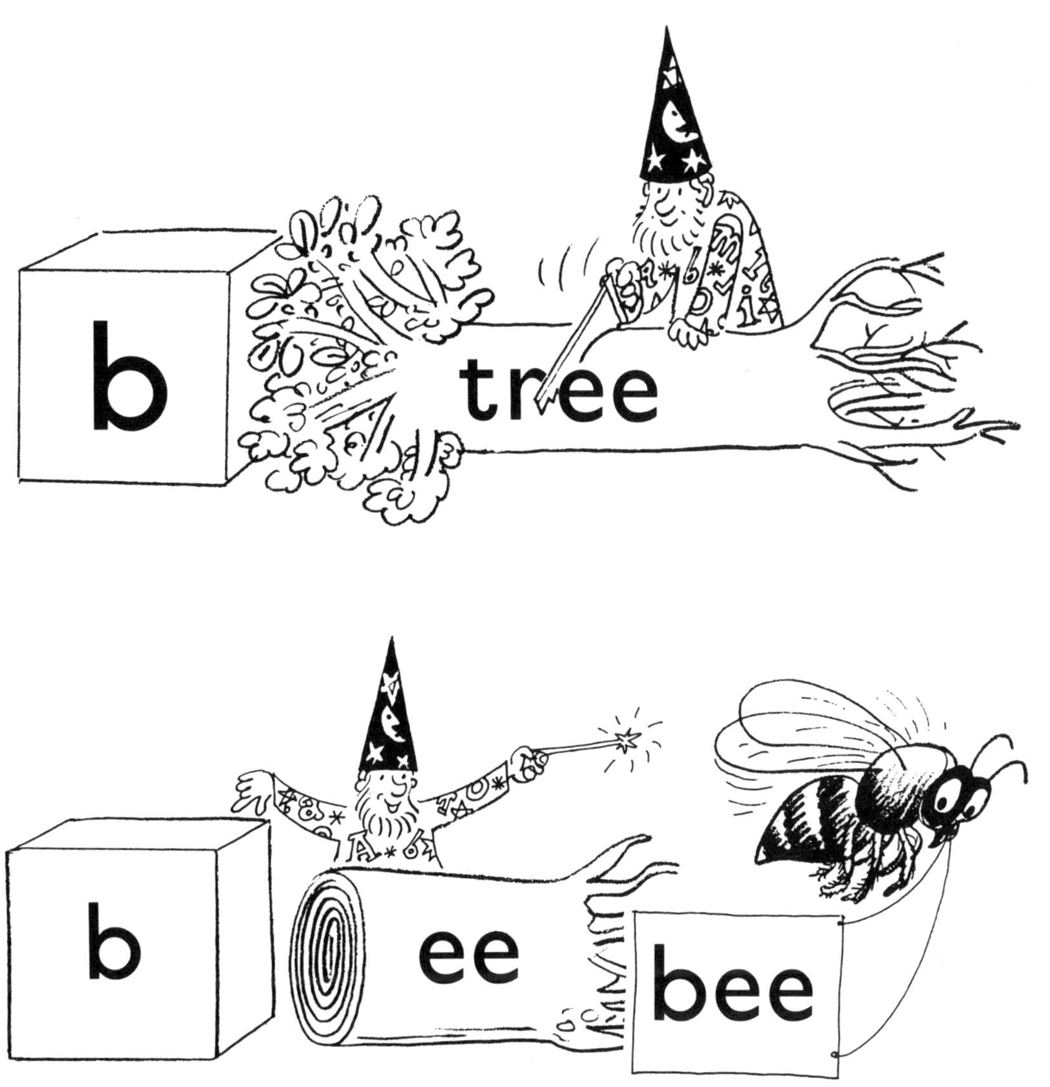
b
tree
b
ee
bee

The children went and played word magic.

saw
and
draw

Saw and draw magic words.

I am a Wizard.
b
h
s
l
m
Dad

s
D
ad

bad	sad	lad	mad
bad	sad	lad	mad
b	s	l	m

Put in the words.

I am ________.
I am ________.
I was ________.

Saw and draw magic words.

h
t
s
y
Mum

tum	sum	hum	yum
tum	sum	hum	yum
t	s	h	y

Put in the words.

!
It is in his
.
3 + 2 =
.

Biff looked at the ______.

First letters

p t l n

Look at the first letters.
Join up the same.

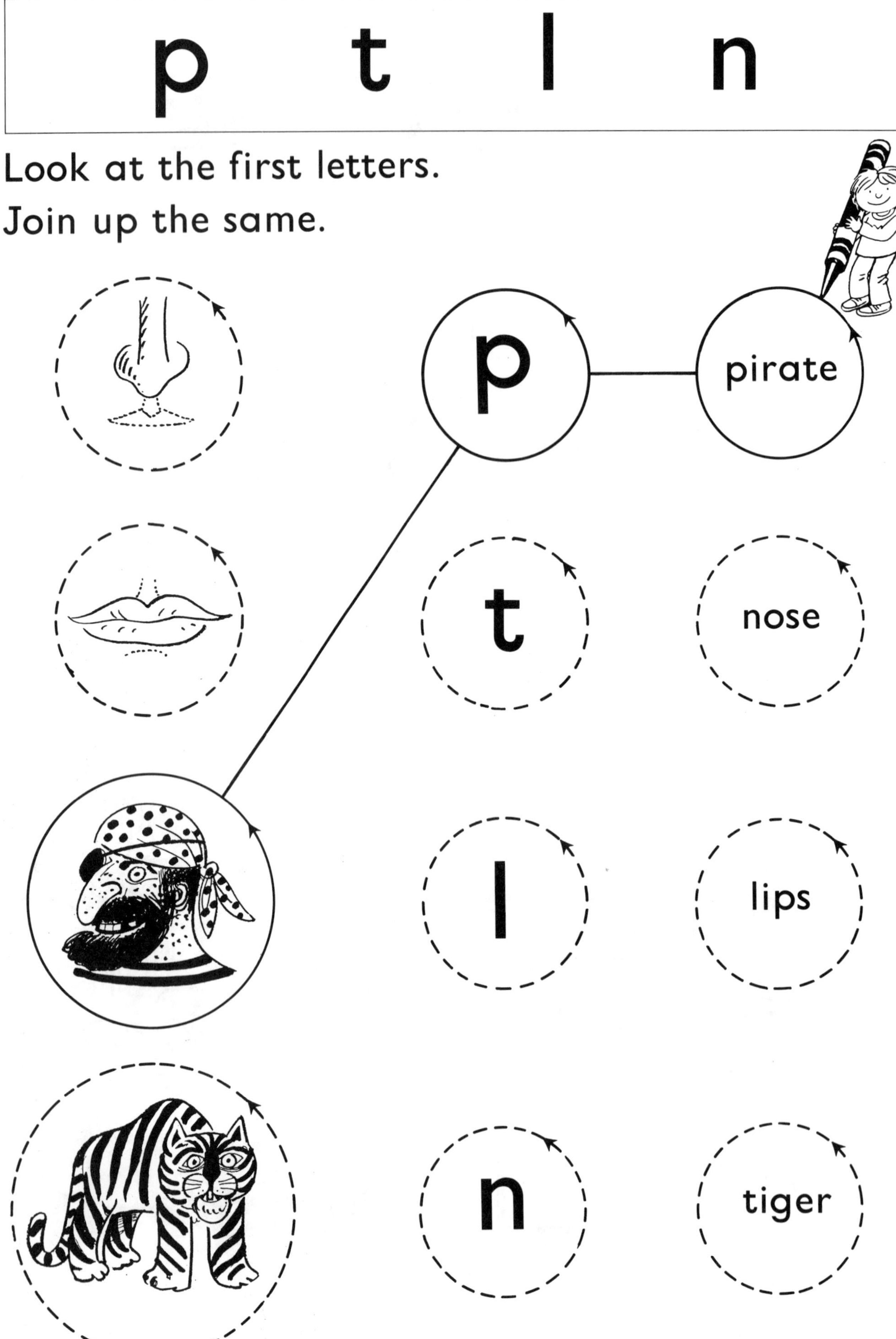
p
pirate
t
nose
l
lips
n
tiger

Saw and draw magic words.

j
dog
l
f
d
og

jog	fog	log
jog	fog	log
j	f	l

Put in the words.

A dog on a
Dad went for a
The children in a

Saw and draw magic words.

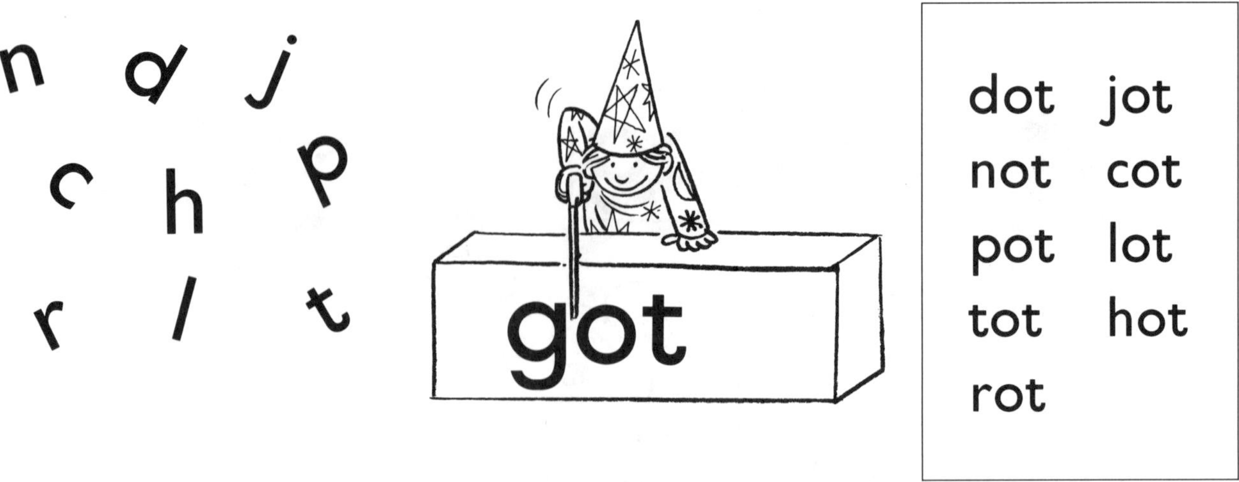
n
a
j
c
h
p
r
l
t
got
dot jot
not cot
pot lot
tot hot
rot

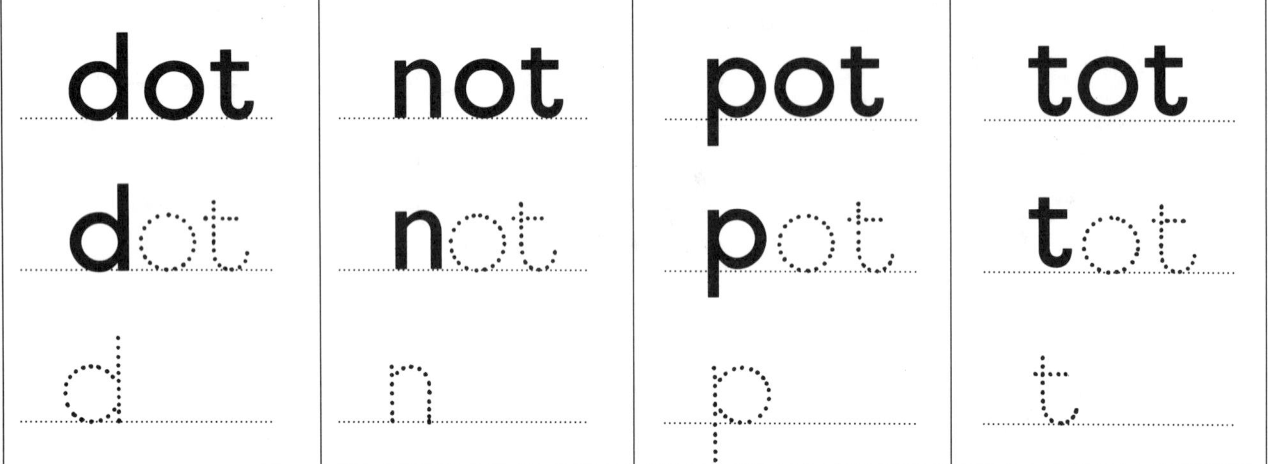
dot
not
pot
tot
dot
not
pot
tot
d
n
p
t

Put in the words.

Mum looked in the ______.
I am ______.
The wizard put a lot in the ______.

First letters.

b	m	c	g

Look at the first letters.

Join up the same.

magnifying
glass

cowboy

bike

girl

Saw and draw magic words.

rug
l
dj
t
m
b

hug
tug
mug
dug
bug

tug	mug	dug	bug
tug	mug	dug	bug
t	m	d	b

Put in the words.

Biff looked at a

________.

Put it in the
________.

Wilma gave Kipper a

________.

Chip gave it a

________.

Wilf gave Dad

a ________.

Saw and draw magic words.

went
t
s
d
r
b

tent
sent
rent
bent
dent
lent

sent	bent	lent	dent
sent	bent	lent	dent
s	b	l	d

Put in the words.

It's ________.
The children played in
a ______.
It was
______.
What a
______.

First letters.

t	l	n	b	m	g	c

Look at the first letters.

Join up the same.

nurse

ball

television

moon

curtains

lorry

goggles

Saw and draw magic words.

get
j p w
n v
m
b y
s l
bet net
jet set
let vet
met wet
pet yet

Put in the words.

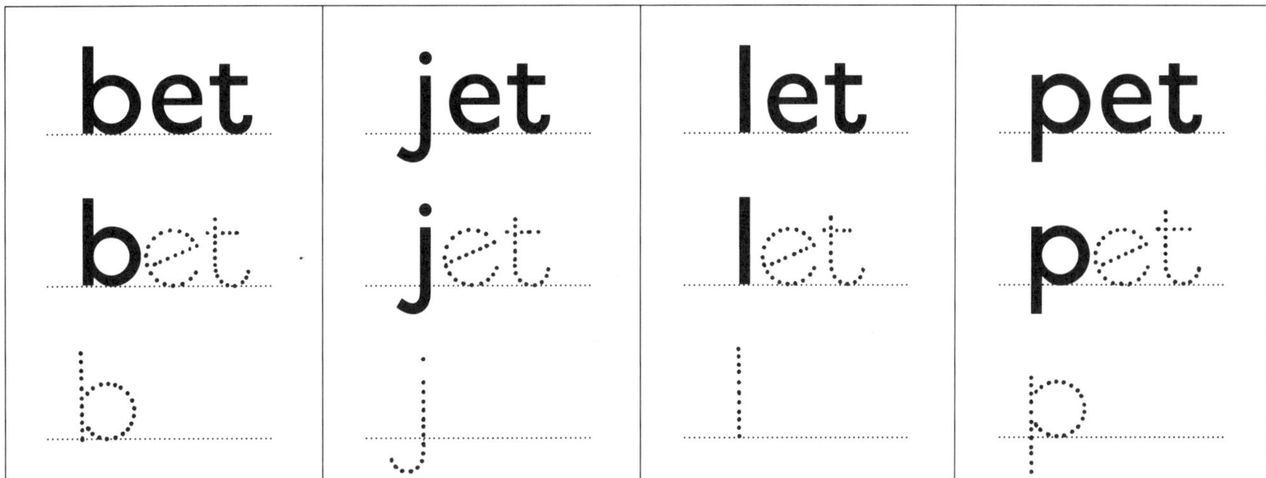
bet jet let pet
bet jet let pet
b j l p

I am ________.	Everyone looked at the ________.	Is it ________?
Floppy is a ________.	Is Chip up ________?	The pet went to the ________.

Saw and draw magic words.

put
h
c
n

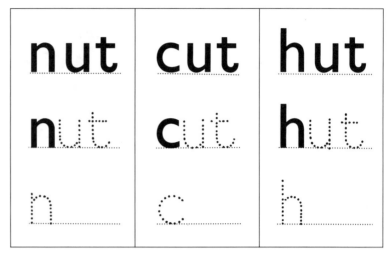

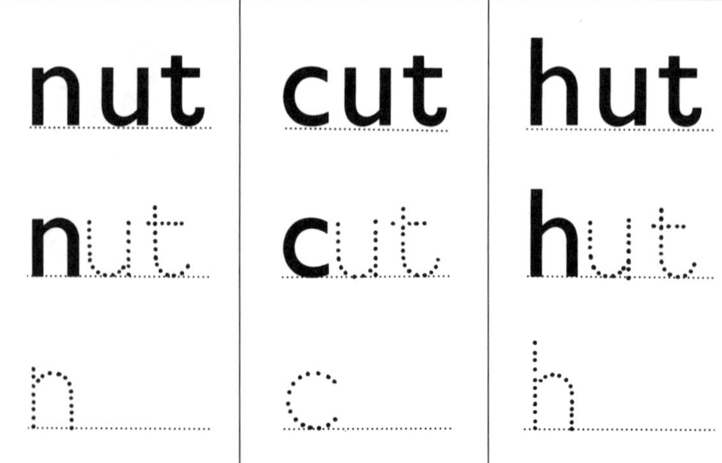
nut cut hut
nut cut hut
n c h

gave

Biff looked in a
________.

c
s
w

wave save cave
wave save cave
w s c

What a
________!

Kipper gave a
________.

He went in a
________.

First letters.

d	k	f	s	r	w

Look at the first letters.
Join up the same.

food

donkey

woman

kangaroo

sock

radio

E.14

Saw and draw magic words.

b
l
t
cross

cr
t
oss

toss	boss	loss
toss	boss	loss
t	b	l

Put in the words.

I am the ________.
What a ________!
Mum gave it a ________.

Saw and draw magic words.

t
h
m
p
stop

st
p
op

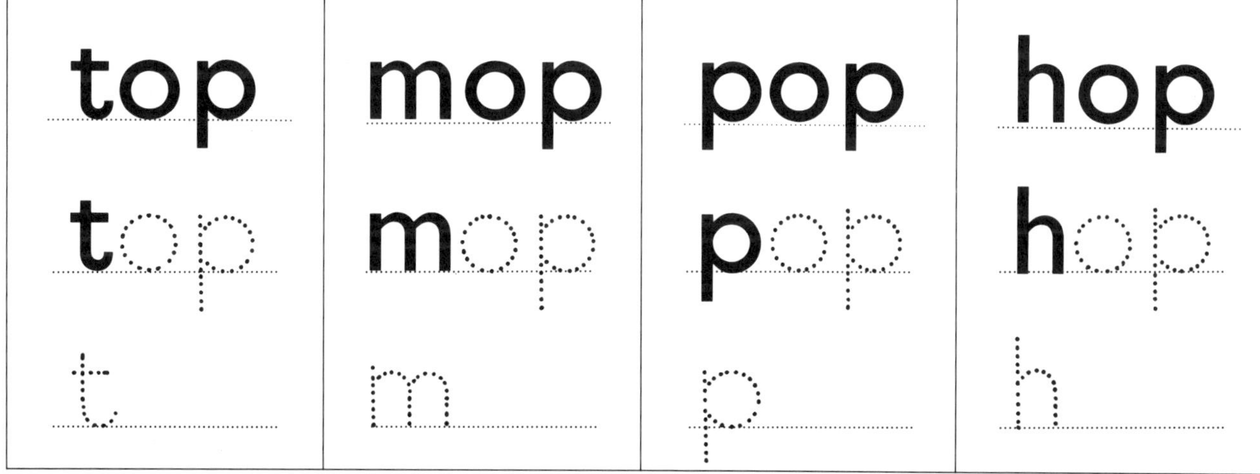
top
mop
pop
hop
top
mop
pop
hop
t
m
p
h

Everyone saw it ________.

Wilf climbed to the ________.

Biff sat on the ________.

E.16

Saw and draw magic words.

Chip
t l z
h r
n
d

zip hip
rip nip
tip dip
lip

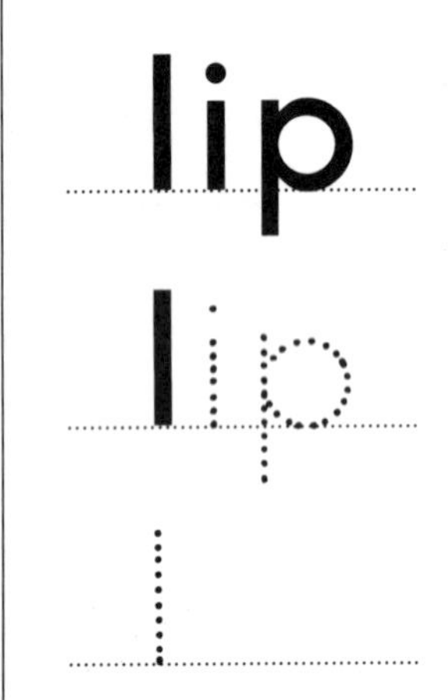
lip
l

dip
d

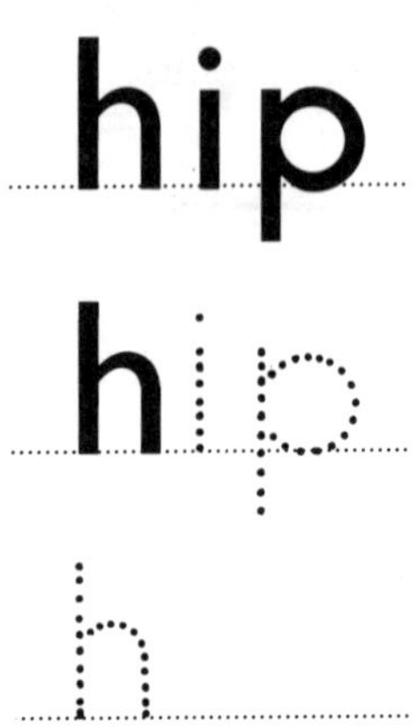
hip
h

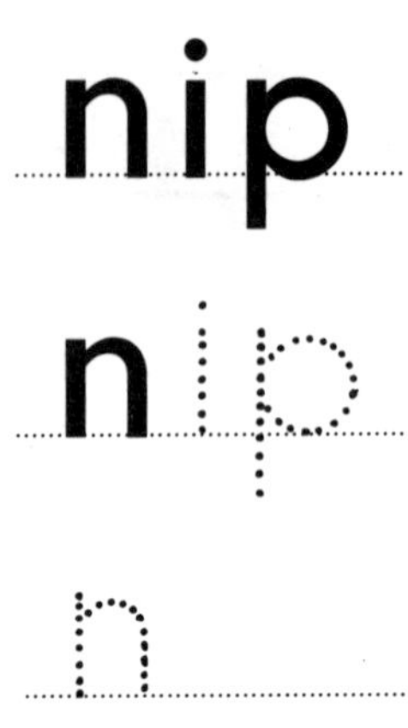
nip
n

Wilf had bumped his ________.

The dog gave the cat a ________.

Wilma climbed up but had a ________.

Kipper pulled at his ________.

Dad went in for a ________.

Kipper cut his ________.